Exploded View

John Griswold, *series editor*

EXPLODED VIEW

Essays on Fatherhood, with Diagrams

DUSTIN PARSONS

The University of Georgia Press *Athens*

Published by the University of Georgia Press
Athens, Georgia 30602
www.ugapress.org
© 2018 by Dustin Parsons
All rights reserved
Designed by Erin Kirk New
Set in Miller Text
Printed and bound by Thomson-Shore
The paper in this book meets the guidelines for
permanence and durability of the Committee on
Production Guidelines for Book Longevity of the
Council on Library Resources.

Most University of Georgia Press titles are
available from popular e-book vendors.

Printed in the United States of America
22   21   20   19   18   P   5   4   3   2   1

Library of Congress Control Number: 2017042883
ISBN: 9780820352879 (pbk. : alk. paper)
ISBN: 9780820352886 (ebook)

For Pascal and Jasper, my constant reminders of good

And for Aimee, who helps me see beauty in the pieces and the whole

....

CONTENTS

Pumpjack

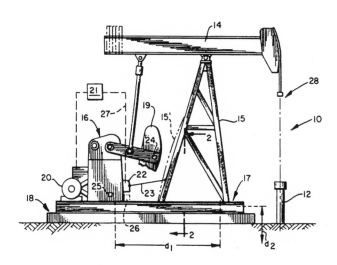

1. This is the tank battery, where the oil ends up. We always start where the oil ends up.

d1. You can gauge it, measure it, pump it, and haul it.

d2. The tank looks like a battery, I told him, and he said he thought so too, and maybe that is where it got its name.

2. It is a single drum tank battery,

2. so maybe it also looks like a drum, he said,

10. and the words skirted into the metal of the tank and around it like
    a skiffing snow.
12. We were surrounded by metal made gray with cold.
14. And that is the pumpjack, he told me, pointing into a field,
    and I guessed that name referred to the machine,
15. as it pumped a stroke up and down the wellhead. He said I'd
    probably be right and that lots of stuff was like that in the oil field.
15'. The gun barrel isn't the barrel of a gun, but a thin, tall tank that
    helps settle contaminants from oil.
16. It looks like the barrel of a gun.
17. That is the pit over there.
18. It was just grass and I didn't see a pit, but a gentle depression rolled
    the prairie, suggesting there might have been one there before, full
    of rotary mud,
19. soft below the surface, shot there from a great discharge fountain.
20. This is the doghouse, this is the pipe rack, so on and so forth, and
    we walked through the field naming things that sounded like the
    things they were.
21. And the snow was snow and it started harder down. Why suddenly
    did every signifier sound and look like its signified?
22. Only for that few minutes we spent there, a prairie dog was a
    prairie dog, and it couldn't be anything more, but when you stepped
    in the prairie dog hole you wished they were not.
23. And wasn't it strange that no word, for that short time, meant
    something else? Chain was almost a linked set of symbols that held

together a sentence and rattled past my cheek pulling my ass along. Grass was brown shoots in dusty thin loam.

24. An oil-field rat was a man many people didn't think acted like a man. An oil-field hand was a man who bored a hole through earth and sky and brought crude forth from it, and oil-field rats rarely went home after performing this divination, but went to the bar, got in fights, and did too many things for which they became rats.

25. Too many heart shots and dice rolling and hard kidding to make sense of the hoolala and the doodlebugging

26. and the simple grunting of the day.

27. Time wasn't a gear, but it turned,

28. and in turning showed an old side and an old side.

Dispatches from the Fifty-First State

The 412 into Tulsa

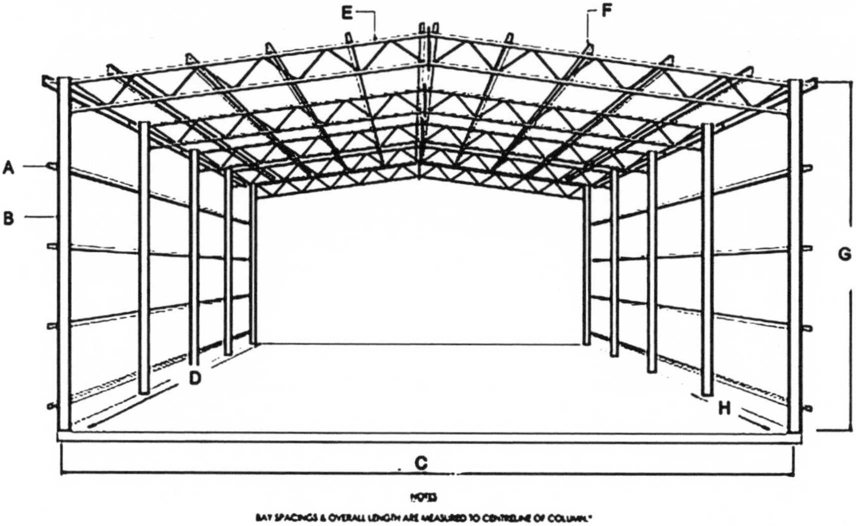
E
F
A
B
G
D
H
C
NOTES
BAY SPACINGS & OVERALL LENGTH ARE MEASURED TO CENTRELINE OF COLUMN."

Figure 1

A. The man didn't know how to weld when they hired him on as a
    welder in the fall of 1973. He simply told the foreman he could
    do it, and he was good help, so the foreman took a chance. Road
    construction shut down, and this was all that was left.
B. The man hadn't worked a highway crew before either, but there he
    was blasting and paving the 412 into Tulsa, the Cimarron Turnpike,
    the entire summer.
C. His wife was pregnant with their first. They moved several hundred
    miles for the job.
D. He drove a scraper most of the day during the summer, smoothing
    the screening or leveling the pad for rebar, and *what it did to the
    kidneys*, he said, how it could *shake a man loose inside*.
E. North Oklahoma looks flat, but what it lacks in hills it makes up for
    in subsurface sandstone and shale.
F. The scrub brush and thistle, the ironweed. Dense pockets of
    stubborn green dotting the browning pasture and farmland.
G. A surprising salt deposit.
H. The grass is prickly. There weren't roots deep enough with all
    that rock.

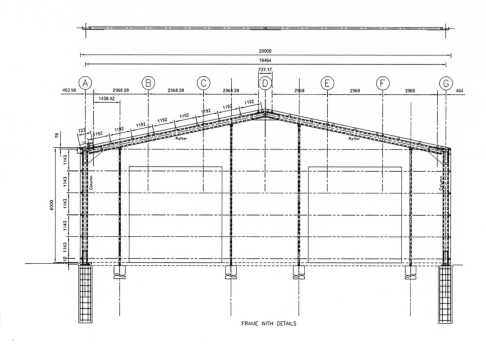

Figure 2

FRAME WITH DETAILS

A. Building a road is about slow advance. One crew is leveling everything in its path, another is laying frames, and another is laying pavement.
B. And the road appears. It is rock and metal rebar and concrete, and they are all rough-edged.
C. In the summer they are sharp and hot, and in the winter they are sharp and cold.
D. His first welding job was to construct the shelter that would take them through the winter.
E. A crew of three scavenged lead-line tubing from a nearby oil-field yard sized with pipe cutters for the frames and discarded tin for walls.
F. The man had practiced on the teeth of drill bits and the blade of the scraper, reinforcing it with new metal. The panels for the walls would latch together so the structure could be erected on location and then disassembled and moved as the season dictated.
G. When finished, the shed was forty feet by twenty-five feet— big enough to house heavy machinery for repair.

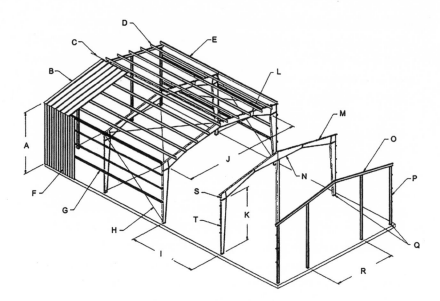

Figure 3

A. The winter in Oklahoma doesn't move in until December at least, and even in 1973, the year he built this first shed, the temperatures hovered in the fifties and forties for highs in October and November, a comfortable temperature to work in.

B. But in December the temperatures could plummet, as they did that year, into the twenties, with wind and snow.

C. By December, then, the shed would need to be complete in order to continue work.

D. Pictures show him in perpetual beard, slim, always suspicious of the camera. Always a flannel and vest on. A messy shock of black hair wind-blown.

E. His draft number got called a few years before, but the war had been scaled back and he was never ordered to basic.

F. That fall, vandals had stripped his vw bug to nothing on location where he'd left it over a weekend. He and the crew crushed it with the heavy machinery and buried it beneath the 412, where it presumably still rests.

G. He was attached to very little.

H. Once they completed the gray corrugated A-frame, they lit a flamethrower big enough to thaw the ground and blew the flame into a fifty-five-gallon drum in the center of the shop.

I. The wind rattled the tin. The walls let the heat waft away. There was always around them the unforgiving cold of machines.

J. The flicker of the torch and welder, that smell of smoldering wire and metal. The electric charge sound bouncing off the tin. "China

Groove" and "Ramblin' Man" on the radio in their trucks, but no radio in the shop—they'd never be able to hear it.

K. He said it was a great time in his life, but like all great things he couldn't do it forever. *It was too hard*, he said. *A great time, but too hard.*

L. The baby was born in the middle of December.

M. The road was not yet finished, but the shed stood when the baby was born.

N. They'd finished the shelter early, by the end of October, and it was a solid shelter that lasted the company he worked for for several years.

O. The company he worked for was only contracted for a portion of the road, and it was a long process.

P. He demystified the road, reduced it to its parts.

Q. The man was proficient in building roads and shelter now, and a man with that many skills might make himself useful in other places.

R. The night before the baby was born he took highway 64 to get to Tulsa on a shopping errand with his very pregnant wife because highway 412 wasn't finished yet. He'd never see it finished, and that was okay. He'd seen the plans, the expectations, the schematics.

S. He'd made a home out of understanding the way a world was laid out on paper. His son would inherit this ability so many years later.

T. There was always a roundabout way, a backcountry highway to the hospital in Cleveland, Oklahoma, the country hospital, when they had to return early so the baby could emerge.

Pumpjack

The enduring image I will always have of the pumpjack is how it takes life. My first encounter was a coyote, its body still reaching for whatever rabbit it chased into the counterweights, the head swiftly separated from the pursuit. My father was checking the well, maintaining the pumpjack, and he came across the carcass when he shut the counterweights down at the engine. I was in grade school, asked to remain in the truck until the machine was at a standstill. That's when my father called me to have a look.

In western Kansas the pumpjack looks like a parishioner in full genuflection among the grasses. To what does it pledge its respect? It points its head low to the well and rises and repeats this gesture for its entire life cycle. It is rare that there is a congregation, but at times one pumpjack can see another in the distance, perhaps part of the same injection field. Their heads are like ball-peen hammers. Corn and wheat grow around the pumpjack, and in the late summer in an irrigated cornfield the pumpjack is the center of its own labyrinth.

I imagined the pumpjack as a living thing when I was young. My father took me to check wells with him, and in the winter I felt sorry for the pumpjack as I might an animal with no shelter. They were often in cattle guard cages. My father implied that certain ones were curmudgeonly, excitable, slow. I didn't name the gesticulating metal, but I wasn't far from it. To me, they were alive.

The drive to the location was a fine one. We left the highway just outside Montezuma, Kansas, to a sandy dirt road maintained by the county. The roads humped in the middle and the truck felt like it might be slipping toward the ditches, unmowed and wild and seemingly bottomless, so we drove the center until we came to a passing truck. There were grater ruts at times where the wash of a short but powerful thunderstorm might sift too much sandy gravel from the road, and the grater that carefully combs the sand back in place struck the hard pan below, giving it the same consistency of rumble strips near construction sites. The wind was low, the temperature was dropping, and it was evening.

From the county roads, the lease roads were nothing more than worn lines connected by a culvert. We entered fields of corn, wheat, and sorghum, the path no wider than our truck, the husks brushing the sides like fingertips. The roads grew increasingly bumpy in the cultivated fields, smoother in the fallow sections.

Below the surface there are rods and pipe and casing that help bring forth oil, gas, and water. It is imperfect and so in need of constant maintenance, which brings roustabouts and pumpers. Much of the pumpjack's life is in its roots, where it has fluid and the cool depth of the earth. It lives to produce. The cottonwoods and the crops continue on, little rain and hardpan of the loam surround it. As with much of what happens in this part of the world, more is going on beneath the ground than above. That which we cannot see we deduce from the personality of the pumpjack. Its color can tell an oilman what company placed it there. Its age tells them about the field's productivity and funding. Its speed tells them about the depth and quality of the crude.

The first lesson in working the oil field: Beware the machinery. A pulling unit can take a life with swift, gruesome abandon. You only need to see a drilling unit and its derrick up close to know the power it can employ to mangle the body. But because the pumpjack looks so little like a machine and so much like an animal in the distance, it lures the living in. It looks so much like a supplicant. So predictable. The cattle guards are not there for show. The coyotes and small game it kills are surprising. The counterweights in the rear drive the crank like the menacing fists of gods. They are meaty guillotines making passes into shallow grave wells.

Beneath the pumpjack in Kansas, Texas, Oklahoma, and the surrounding states is the Mid-Continent Oil Field, the largest crude field in North America, first drilled in 1892 in Neodesha, Kansas. But after the initial boom, with the need to extract the oil in other than natural ways, the pumpjack became a fixture in the fields in the 1920s. They bore little resemblance to the modern nodding donkeys that dot the landscape now, with hand-hewn logs for beams and the look of a teeter-totter with a great wooden wheel at one end. They're all but gone now, long since relegated to the boneyards or eaten through. It wouldn't be until the 1950s that the pumpjacks became the metal horses we know now.

I stared at the coyote's body for some time. The sun was nearly down, a handful of pencil-thin clouds masking its exit in the west. This was a grazing field, and I could hear the cattle lowing in the distance; the tall prairie grasses that had been allowed to flourish were chattering like an off-air station in the background. My father went about the business of checking the pumpjack and well, greasing the massive machine. It was close to time to go home. We'd been in the truck for the better part of a day, and though this time with my dad was precious, I was ready to go home.

But I wasn't ready to leave the coyote. The surprise with the coyote was the lack of blood. The body could have been sleeping, burying its head in the dust. The coat was gray and brown, coarse and short. An accomplished hunter, the coyote was not stricken with mange, not gaunt. He was a long animal, a formidable predator, clean sharp claws adorning its tattered paws. The tail hair waved in the breeze, so clean. I stepped closer. Little patches of black in the pelt. Some of the hair was lighter at the tips, darker at the base. One could not have seen him in the prairie grasses were he to retreat to safety. The counterweight rested in the ground, its flat end against the neck, and the absurdity of a circus tombstone came to my mind.

My father's words: *This is what happens when you get too close.*

There is an ecosystem there, in the base of the pumpjack, where the I-beams rest like rails on a sled. Small lizards in southwest Kansas, near Ulysses, lie prone and flat on the hot metal. Field mice make their way along the insides of the beams like it's an interstate system. Rabbits burrow into the sheeting of pebbles where the loose gravel is easy digging.

Crabgrass lines the edges of the I-beams on the ground. Nightshade, mustard weed, fireweed (and the resultant tumbleweed), wild carrot. Anything that can survive the chemicals in constant circulation.

Snakes were always a step away, coiled or burrowed in the cool gravel. Mainly bull snakes, little garters, but occasionally a rattler might make its home there.

Robins and swallows nested in the horse head, especially in gas pumpjacks that run only a portion of the day. If the engine was housed in an open-sided port or a small shed, beware the birds' anger at someone disturbing their babies in spring. Spiders in the corners. Hawks on the walking beam searching for prey. The cattle rub against the fencing with each visit.

From the gearbox I've cleaned whole nests of rats. They enter through conduit holes in the bottom of battery boxes and rectifiers. They enter through the open seams of metal, the rusted corners and bent lids. There is a whole history mice exploit in order to make their nests. The smell is fetid and dizzying. It is rare to have to evict a rat, but the babies are often dumped from the box unceremoniously.

The first nest I cleared, I picked it up with gloved hands and set it in a ditch for the parents to find. The ditch was shallow, the grass brown and low, the nest easy to spot. The nest had the shape of the gear box at its base—wide but shallow—and had been woven together in such a way that it held that shape in my hands. I could feel it move with the babies inside, but I could barely see them under the protective top layer of grasses.

I returned to seal up the holes with silicone to keep rats from reentering. At the end of the day, as we drove the lease road to the highway, I looked over at the nest in the sun, the babies still buried in the scraps of paper and foliage, and thought how little I could do for them.

When I was old enough, during my return trips from college, my father took me on as an oil-field hand for his very small company. He installs electrical systems to underground pipe and keeps the pipe from corroding by diverting the negative charges that occur naturally underground to a series of sacrificial anodes buried alongside the well. My job was installing the ground wire, which ran from the wellhead where the horse head was, through the base of the pumpjack, and to the rectifier at the back of the pumpjack. The first time I made that trek through the pumpjack, I felt like I was doing something illegal. I'd been warned so many times, even with the machine off, not to go through the pumpjack, but there I was spooling the heavy-gauge wire beneath the metal to pin it in place.

Some pumpjacks run on diesel engines so loud it is difficult to talk on location. It offers some comfort that the noise is an indication of its lethal grind. They have a long lever on the outside of the housing as a brake, and the engine can be powered down after the brake has been set.

I checked a gas well once that wasn't running, took the meter readings on the rectifier at a box a safe distance from the pumpjack's moving parts and recorded them in the book. I pulled on the wires to see that the connections were still solid. The day was windy, and the loudest sound was a thrum of highway traffic half a mile from location. One can start imagining, after some time alone, sounds coming from corn- and wheat fields, the rustling of which hits just the right tone. The wind through barbed wire whistles. At any time these might also have been in the background as I recorded my readings.

Late summer days in southwest Kansas have their own glory. The day is hottest at four, but by six the wind and the increasing shade cools a sweaty back. Boots don't feel so oppressive, and with supper approaching, each checked well was one step closer to home. The cottonwoods and elms blink their leaves in the distance in small untamed groves surrounding creek beds and terrain too mottled to farm. There is often a smell of fresh-turned earth.

I turned around to close the rectifier box on that day and found the pumpjack running, silent, behind me. I remembered an old joke that applied to pumpjacks: What is always running, but can never leave? I'd never known it had kicked on as per its programmed schedule, and the counterweights fluttered behind me like a butterfly.

At night as kids we waded through the boneyards of the oil-field companies, looking for whatever we could find. Rich and I combed one machine shop yard specifically to steal the silver bulldog from the hood of a Mack truck. We didn't have any cutters, so Rich stood on the bumper, his powerful body rocking the hood ornament back and forth, forward and back with violent jerks, working the mounting loose. He looked like he might be pulling in a shark in an offshore fishing expedition, the way he worked for a few pulls, rested, renewed the tugging contest until the piece finally parted with its mount, releasing Rich as well to the ground, where he held up the dog like a receiver verifying a catch.

Parts of the pumpjack lay in those machine shops around the towns I lived in as a child. They were all oil-field towns: Hays, Ness City, Hoisington. In the yards of the machine shops, the welding sheds, the petroleum companies, the service and supply companies, there were the familiar horse heads, the walking beam, the cranks. They were often in poor form, rusting or in various stages of reconstruction. They looked like beaten mules, draft horses gone lame. Valves and casing, pipes and pumps, the heavy metal discard of the oil field. We'd been a generation seeing these pieces in machine shop yards, seeing the missing pieces of our fathers likewise upon return home. Men with fingers numbering less than ten, men with no toes on one foot. I had a neighbor who had lost his left arm, and I watched as his beautiful (to me as a child) blonde wife put on his coat in winter or opened beers for him as they sat under the safety of an opened garage on summer evenings together. I was lucky, I remember thinking even then. My father was still whole.

My childhood was full of the pumpjack. Little League sponsorships, free hats and coffee mugs from the companies with whom my father did business. A man in town had a miniature pumpjack in his yard, and though I can't remember for sure, I think it was pumping a water well. Nearly every oil-field company uses the pumpjack as its symbol. If they do not, then it is the oil derrick. It is backlit by the setting sun, the horse head held high like a hammer poised to strike a rail tie.

The pumpjack is a symbol because it most easily sticks out along the prairie. In the fields it rises above the rest of the foliage except for the rare grove of cottonwoods or locusts eyebrowing a creek. It is a symbol because it keeps its head down and works, because we all want that kind of dedication. In the pumpjack, we all find our desire for focus.

And indeed some of the men in town look like pumpjacks. They have the willowy tensile strength of cables running through their backs and arms. They are always hunched over. Faces like shovels, arms coated in sun and oil and grease they haven't the time or inclination to take off before they gather themselves from their work trucks to have a beer at The Shack. Their pants are spotted black and blue, the drill hands and the pulling unit hands, the men that have to put the pipe in the ground and drag it out when there is a problem. They even move like the pumpjack: slow, even pace around the pool table, down the street, but one nearly feels inclined to believe that for all their movement they are in the same place. They guard their beer at the bar with their arms. They don't look backlit by the sun. They don't look romantic.

That night I climbed the dead pumpjack in the yard, mounting it like a bull rider. The boneyard was just off the highway leading into town. It was fenced off with welded metal pipes three feet high. They stood more like declarations of property than warnings to keep out, and I looked out from atop the pumpjack, the first one I'd ever climbed, and saw the oil-field town at night. The pulling unit crews, despite the darkness, were coming in one at a time, their trucks and rigs coated in rotary mud and crude. They unloaded from the trucks and staggered wearily into the shop before heading home. The cement trucks, finished filling the drilled holes, were parked like sleeping elephants across the highway in an abandoned field. The houses didn't start for another half mile to the south—all around us were metal shed shops, open gravel lots with heavy machinery, the detritus of subterranean exploration. Below me, the warm memory of the sun radiated from the black paint of the tired pumpjack, and the boys called for me to come along. And I did.

Years later, in the summer of 1995, Rich lost his father in the oil field. Dan was a machinist and welder as well as a garbage man in the mornings. I'd worked for him for a time in high school just a few years before, picking up garbage in the surrounding small towns. He was doing repair work on a pumpjack when the weights of the head came loose, crushing him.

Rich and I retreated days after the funeral (which I missed while working in Nebraska as a crop scout) to the blade platform of a windmill just outside of town to drink a case of beer and hope we didn't plummet to our own demises. The windmill is its own kind of pumpjack, a vacuum machine. The spine-numbing water tumbles from the exit valve with the metallic mineral taste I remember from garden hoses and the water my grandparents drank. The pump and rotary were long broken, wood eaten through in the tower, metal blades missing like pulled teeth. The sound of the pipes rattling when another breath of air propelled the fan face and the water drew up sounded like wind chimes located on the porch of Hades, so we employed the brake for the evening. The cows, for which the stock tank was supplied by the mill, would have to make do the following day.

From the platform we could see the grid layout of the country roads. Pumpjacks bowed in the distance. I don't remember what I said. What could I say? Dan had done a dangerous job, worked with weight and motion. His job was to tie them together, and sometimes the problems were too great to fix. Old parts, mismatched pairings. Few were rewarded for trusting what rested above them.

The evening went on and we got drunk. The power of that weight occurred to me during the dusk. Dan must never have known it was coming, and probably, it was my hope, didn't suffer much. Rich told me he had already started heading out to location because he felt like something might be amiss. More a feeling his dad would need another pair of hands to do the job. Nothing so much as what he encountered.

Rich never cried. He'd had enough. We talked about the times he and I worked for his father, riding on the back of the trash truck, kicking "fruit field goals" into the back when we should have been working. We talked about his career as a welder now, and how he did the same sort of work his father did. I don't want to remember the exact conversation. I don't want to approximate it. I'd do a poor job if I tried, and it wouldn't matter much. What mattered is that we saw the sun come up even though we were both exhausted. We finished the beer, made it down without hurting ourselves, and wandered back to town to take our places.

Years earlier, after my encounter with the coyote, my father, sometime during those days he took me along to check wells, gave me my first taste of beer. Coors, from the can. He only had a few, and at the time nobody really thought twice about drinking a few beers as they drove home from work. I jabbed at the opening, a small sip when it was passed to me. It tasted bitter and metallic. Cool but not cold. It tasted like a bolt might taste had I put it in my mouth. That's what it felt like too, like I was finally taking in what it meant to work with the dangerous metal, the moving arms and fists of pumpjacks. Out the window pumpjacks bowed and rose in the distance. It was dark by then, and we were on the sandy dirt road home. A rooster tail of dust rose up in our wake. It was only a sip, but a sip was enough.

Harvest

The wheat is planted in the winter, in the spring, in the hard ground, in the cover, in the continuously tilled and turned field, in the stubble from the corn from last year, in the rows of chaff that remain like the prickly hairs on the chin denied the razor. The grain is planted by tractor, tucked in with a prow and a drop and a grating for cover. There is nitrogen. There is water. More than once there are prayers.

There is inflorescence. There is anthesis. Whole fields go green overnight, a cult of green, a germination exposed and exploding. There is sun and there is thunder, irrigation and insurance for hail and wind and drought and flood. One in four years there is hearty bushel. There is too early to tell and too late to cut. The grain emerges and there is milk development and dough development and the ripening and the rusting and the insect populations and the weed problems and more chemicals. There is the hard kernel and the drooping straw and the rustling in the breeze that gives away the time to cut, and there is feeling the heads between finger and thumb and the way it falls apart on contact like a sepia-stained ghost.

There is knee-high by the Fourth of July and custom cutters and zerks to grease and headers to clean. Combines to drive, grain bins to fill, and grain trucks to haul, and they rest in the fields until it is dry enough and then cut and haul until it is too dark to see their way. There are sandwiches behind the wheel when the cutting starts, and there is coffee, too much coffee even for kids hired on, and there is a blind eye to driver's licenses or lack thereof. There is the sun, always in the eyes, and the heat of the July field rising up through the open windows of ancient pickups with no air. There are the old men. They wear long sleeves. There are the young men, and they cut the sleeves off. The dirt rises from the combines, the grain dust too, and it leeches every inch of body and mouth and nose and ears, and they all know that the sleeves can't be returned.

The grain carts to the trucks to the roads to the highways. The highways to the towns to the out-of-the-way majesty of twenty-bin grain elevators. There are Texas houses, auger lifts, the swirling mass of collected grain. There is the pit set flush with metal grate, where they find me with a shovel, the two high school girls working the scales and recording the weights in the long green and lined log books. There is no go until they thumb up, and then there is the power takeoff and the lifting of the bed and the release of the grain. In the night there are dreams of grain falling unending, pushing out all other dreams, and the sound is a lullaby, a particular white noise, maybe a golden noise, high pitched, the bells of a child's toy from memory, the rattling of teeth and hands, the numbing of nerve endings; and this is a full day. There are no masks, so there are kerchiefs and torn shirts for makeshift aerators.

There is the classmate who is a fuckup, not allowed to work his father's garage, and the older kid, the one who graduated a few years ago but hasn't left town, who will never leave town. They carry shovels too, they scrape the bins, they smoke outside the elevator entrances dangerously close to the grain particles, the little remaining gift the grain has to offer, that could combust but never do.

The trucks line up and there is music and there are beers exchanged, and it is the Fourth of July and there is the work until farmers can no longer see. It almost never lands on the Fourth of July but here it is and the trucks are a trickle and there is the Texas house, atop the bins, and glass walls, so you take one of the girls upstairs, the concrete stairway that snakes around bin twelve, the outside, narrow enough for only one at a time, and it winds around and there is the exhaustion but the beers in pockets and after a time the stairway, the dark, dark stairway opens to the room with the windows, and the catwalk that extends outside, and there is the open night, and the view of the entire town and the brief anxiety about just how high this grain elevator stands. There could be whole downtown buildings below. There could be fifteen trucks stacked atop one another and not reaching the top. And there are cars cruising Main and the high school girl who only wants the beer and the time to look out, to see the sudden blossoms come and go.

Later, the older kid is convicted of rape, the fuckup is killed on his motorcycle, and there is the realization that their fate wasn't so clear. There were the words, the thoughts to their families. The high-schooler is married, the elevator bought and sold more than once. There were streetlight highways and dark estuaries that faded off into the night, and the cracking of a firework against the sky outlining the otherwise darkened streets. There were roman candles shot out of cars, the rapid pop of Black Cats, the submerged sound of an M-80 unleashed. There were rockets, flares, worms, sparklers. The darkness of such a small town, all its secrets under the light. It was a first job, and I thought they'd all be like that. Thought they'd all end in such billows. Below there were infinite grains, above the bursting of pyrotechnics. The beer might be there too, and the night, and the next day and the rain holding off and the town receding after the final red explosion.

Transmission

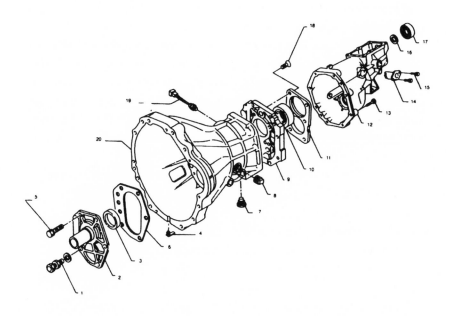

1. We decide that the best way is to drop the transmission onto my dad's chest and let him hold it there while I replace the seal.
2. We could have found some padding, I suppose, an old mattress or the seat to a '56 Willys sitting in his shop, but this seems faster, and

besides, we'll have a man who has his ass behind the weight when it's time to put the transmission back.

3. He lowers it as slowly as he can, but it plants itself on his sternum like a funnel cloud kissing ground.

4. The inside of a transmission when the housing is disassembled from the transfer case looks like the bottom of a bell, but with a grinding set of gears for a clapper hidden by the torque converter.

5. It oozes fluid like a sore, and the old seal is all but gone already. What is left has crusted to the edges of the housing, and I scrape it off with a putty knife.

6. There is my father, the weight of the transmission bearing down on his chest.

7. He breathes shallowly, looks around the transmission at me to direct what to do next.

8. I lay the seal along the housing's edge.

9. I've greased it with transmission fluid.

10. When I was a kid he worked all day long and answered phones all evening as the pulling unit crews checked in.

11. He was never off. Never done.

12. He tells me the transmission isn't too heavy when I ask him later.

13. About one hundred pounds, he says. It was more than that.

14. We put the transmission back.

15. He bench-presses the weight while I grip it as best I can and help.

16. We slide the housing to the transfer case like putting a cap on a pen. We attach the output shaft, replace the bolts.

17. We are silent.
18. On my father's shirt is the Rorschach print of grease from the transmission.
19. When he is working it is a crooked river.
20. When he reaches for a bolt on the floor and his arms open, it is a mushroom cloud, a tornado. A furious ringing bell.

Dispatches from the Fifty-First State

Statistical Populations

- In 1992, nine counties huddled in southwestern Kansas voted to secede from the rest of the state, so disgusted were they with the state legislature's thirty-two-mill levy on education per student, and the counties in question made a shape like a question mark.
- I have called myself a Kansan all my life, even though statistically I have lived only half my life within its borders, a higher percentage than in any other state, but still a statistic that doesn't reflect which years that 50 percent encompasses.
- Statistically a marriage ends every three seconds in the United States, and many of those are strung together within milliseconds during the day like ridges on a rumble strip, so that late in the night, in bed or shivering on the couch, perhaps an entire minute might go by without so much as a thought of leaving.
- Statistically about 85 percent of my extended family lives in Kansas, only 40 percent of my immediate childhood family, and 0 percent of my current immediate family.

Surveys and Experiments

- In 2013, 13 percent of adults said in a Rasmussen Report poll that if their state declared itself sovereign, they would remain quiet, wait, and see what happened.
- In every one hundred respondents, the sampling error of plus or minus three floats like neighborhood ghosts across the numbers, communing with the audience.
- Representatives from all fifty states have advocated and pushed forward legislation in favor of secession at one time or another since 2008, the same year we elected our first black president.
- Total wheat production has dropped by approximately 50 percent in the last fifteen years. Charts show a steady decline in production in the years since 1990 in yield and in acres planted and harvested, with occasional plummets that look like lies on a polygraph.
- 13.2 percent of Kansas residents do not identify on the 2014 census as white. The national average is 22.6 percent.
- Of that 13.2 percent, a vast majority do not live in western Kansas, the primary part of the state that wished to secede.
- The price of a barrel of oil in 1992 was $19.25, and it currently stands at $42.00.

Data Analysis

- A *state* is a region of a country when lowercase and a country when capitalized. In case anyone thinks grammar doesn't matter.

- Western Kansas taxable revenue that might be withheld from the rest of the state in oil and gas alone was estimated by a Dallas newspaper in 1992 to stand at around $70 million.
- Once national magazines picked up the Kansas secession story, organizers began negotiating with then–Kansas governor Finney. As the Hawthorn Effect suggests, simply viewing a process changes it.

Probability Theory

- One reason given consistently against new state formation is that fifty-one stars would be awkward on the flag. This is, by far, the stupidest reason to reject secession from a state.
- The statistical probability of a successful bid for secession from a state stands at about nil in the United States due to *Texas v. White* (1869), unless there is all-out revolution.
- Another reason given consistently against new state formation is that it sets a dangerous precedent for communities who disagree with their legislators. This is a better reason.
- Secession from the Union and secession of one part of a state from the rest are given no appreciable distinction in form or deed according to authorities.
- There is a connection between the cohesiveness of a people and the cohesiveness of their state. That they might disagree is common. That they might resist schism in favor of compromise is becoming more and more rare.

- It is uncomfortable to suspect that statistics can lead to an assumption. To some sort of conclusion. To a theory of probability. I imagined
- my life to be more than a predictable summation of what came before.
- Maybe numbers, like a gray celebration,
- tell me that home and memory can still be reconcilable.

Solar Array

Part 1: Windshield Time

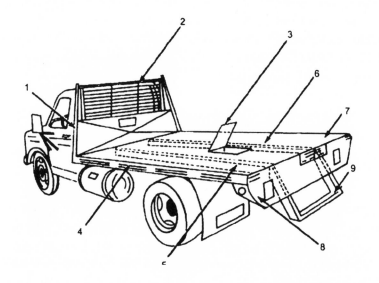

1. On the day we left, my father told me that some marriages can stand a little breathing room.
2. We were working nearly four hours to the southwest in Grant County near Ulysses, Kansas, where we'd rented a small home from a potato farmer.
3. Our job was to change out about 120 solar regulators on the gas wells all over the county.
4. Many were severely neglected, my father said, and would require full disassembly in the field.
5. This was a job too big for a commute.
6. I guess he told me about the breathing room in case I had any worries that he was trying to escape.
7. I didn't have those worries, but the cab of the truck did feel smaller suddenly, our bags and pillows and my books crammed into every corner of the crew cab.
8. There isn't much music radio in western Kansas, only a few country stations, and my father considers country music one rung above "stranglin' cats," so there was silence. He spent a lot of time like that, behind the windshield driving to a location by himself, in the quiet, and I could never understand how he didn't want to talk all the time when he wasn't alone.
9. Oil-field hands call it *windshield time*, and the hum and vibration of the passenger seat can feel so hypnotic one could conceivably sleep the entire four-hour trip once a subject like marriage was broached.

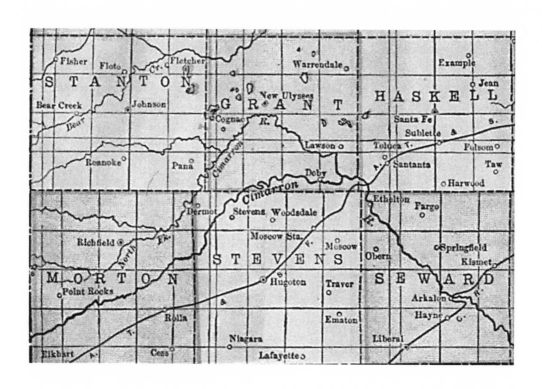

★ Rattlesnake and sand country, Grant County shares more characteristics with New Mexico and Texas than it does with our home in midwestern Kansas.

◉ The drive includes so many straight-line highways from which one can see for miles on the horizon line.

● Pumpjacks teetered in the distance, grain elevators stuck their fingers to the sky like a salute.

● The grass was brown, sizzled down to French-fried curls from the ground.

● Small towns popped up when we weren't looking, nestled into the small valleys along the road: Jetmore, Hanston, Montezuma, Sublette, Satanta, Hugoton, Rolla.

— Many were unincorporated, and others had an ice cream place, a pizza or hamburger joint, oil-field chemical outfits and roustabout services, pulling-unit yards and parking lots in front of auto garages big enough to take in a pulling-unit rig, machine shops and John Deere dealerships.

H The spine was the highway, and the towns were usually bones spreading outward like a snake's skeleton.

〜 Wind farms and factory farms mingled like nosy neighbors in the open areas between towns.

⬮ It was the open, flat landscape that made one feel so small, that made everything look so vacant. But it teemed with life beneath the prairie grass, wheat, corn, alfalfa, and cattle.

(New to Rent) A rambler with charm located on the northwest corner of a potato field (all the boilers you can pick). This dandy is located just outside the town limits of Ulysses, in Grant Co. Dish network hookups if you can keep the dish level and pointed south in the regular wind and thunderstorms of the area. Dirt yard means no lawn care for tenant, and a clothesline keeps the energy costs down. Original carpet and appliances. Window unit in living room. Extra amenities include open floor plan, floor mattresses, and a dog.

List Price:	$200/month
Property Type:	Single Half Family
Style:	Rambler Ranch
City:	Ulysses
County:	Grant
Est. Sq. Ft.:	350, but it feels cozier
Bedrooms:	2
Full Baths:	1
Year Built/Age:	Depression Era
Taxes:	You Bet

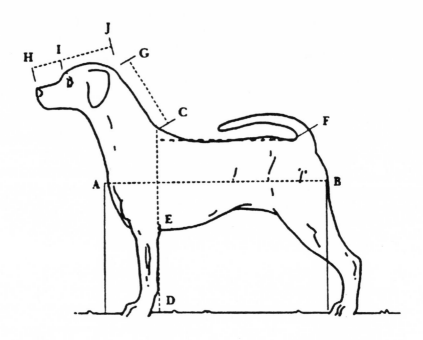

A–B: He appeared out of the fields, and we called him Rock.

C–D: One of the first nights we had him, he crawled onto the back of my father's truck and ate through about $100 worth of 8-gauge wire, and my father didn't try to kill him.

C–G: My father had a soft spot for animals, and still does, feeding all the cats in the neighborhood despite my mother's protestations.

D–E: A mix between a Doberman and a Lab, he was a glossy black like a felt-top poker table, with a mutt's damaged paws and an abandoned dog's hunger.

C–E: He always showed up at the end of the day after we returned from work, strolling in about dinner time, begging on the porch.

F–C: When my father and I went to dig potatoes one afternoon, Rock got hold of one and began eating it, then another.

J–H: We had to call him in from the field once he discovered that they were so easy to dig up.

J–I: At night, after we'd fed him and we had returned to the house to read, watch television, and sleep, Rock slept on our porch.

H–I: Rock wasn't the kind of dog that could come inside, so every morning he was gone, only to return the following evening.

Part 3: The Solar Array

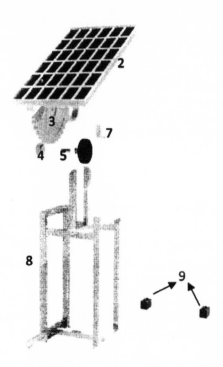

Figure 1: Solar Array

2. The solar arrays were our primary job. So many of them had been left in the open, unattended, for years. The blowing sand and the relentless sun, not to mention the wildlife, had made them little more than small shade for animals.

3. We were allowed to keep the panels and the scrap we found if they couldn't be easily repaired. The panels, while seeming to be the most delicate part of the operation, were damn hearty. With proper batteries installed, wire reconnected, and a good "dusting off," most of the panels still ran quite well. Sometimes the pumpers would turn the arrays off, fray a cord when they drove over them, steal panels thinking they could get them to work on other contraptions, or just leave them to the elements even when they saw one damaged.

4. The job of the solar array was to generate power to store in the batteries, using that power to push a small current to the pipeline below the ground, where the natural charge was negative. The positive charge the array sent would ensure minimal corrosion on the buried pipelines, saving the company money in repairs. And, as a correlative, be better for the environment in the short run.

5. Each array we came to was a jigsaw puzzle, but over the course of the summer I was getting good at putting them together. The electronics were easy, but the metal was too hot to touch with a bare hand, the battery boxes often had huge rats' nests in them, and at night, after a day of sun and wind and the dirt that was hurled at me, I blew dark

snot from my nose, washed dunes from my hair, and scrubbed my hands raw trying to get the grease from my arms.

7. Each array had a small regulator that helped keep the charge even and reduced surges. These were often damaged too.

8. The metal frames weighed about as much as a piece of scaffolding. Each of the four panels regularly required tightening unless we were scrapping the whole array. In those cases, I disassembled them and stacked them on the trailer like playing cards.

9. The batteries were almost always fried. We packed them up and delivered them to be recycled. A few batteries were salvageable, but too many had simply been there past their reasonable lifetime.

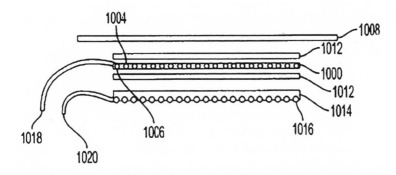

Figure 2: Solar Panel

FIGURE 2: SOLAR PANEL

1000: I'd always thought power required burning, explosion, force: there is simply nothing passive about wind, gas, and coal.

1004: And when you see the process of transitioning power from sunlight to energy, you do see a magnificent (and not at all passive) process taking place called the photovoltaic effect. To the human eye and ear, though, there is nothing but quiet absorption.

1006: That was the gas field workday for me—the hum of wind, the sounds of rustling yucca and chaff, a distant electric charge of heavy trucks on the highway that only entered my consciousness when I stopped what I was doing and wanted to notice it.

1008: I too took in the sun, pointed my face south and took it in.

1012: On some mornings, my second cousin who lived close to our rented house came over to work with us, and took a shot of tequila he kept stored in our freezer that poured out like syrup.

1014: Every couple of weeks we went back for a Saturday/Sunday with mom, me sleeping, my father exchanging the scrap we hauled back for working panels and batteries we had stored in his shop.

1016: When the rare rain fell, it made a muddy mess of the entire county. Two high school girls got stuck in the mud on a country access road one day, a green Chevy Cavalier up to the wheel wells in thick sandy mud.

1018: Dad and I were behind the car, pushing the bumper, then trying to rock it back and forth, forward and back, trying to catch hold of something beneath the loose mud.

1020: The driver gunned it when I was behind the tire and I ended up fully mudded from head to toe. But that was the push it needed, and the girls were able to fight their way out of the mire.

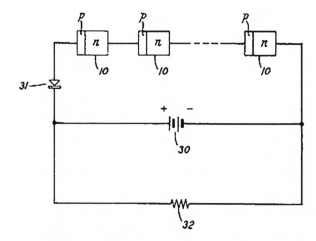

Figure 3: Solar Cell

FIGURE 3: SOLAR CELL

1. If I was already gone in my mind, my memory knew better.
2. There are moments in my life that feel like stored bright energy, waiting there to be summoned to keep me going, to define my direction, to help me make decisions.
3. This summer was one of those moments.
4. Beneath the house and the solar panels and the dirt and the sun, there is this peace.
5. It is the same feeling I get when I hike by myself, knowing that if I wandered off the path nobody would know where I went; when I look out at a backyard, at an empty field, at the countryside, and I remember a wrench in my hand, taking apart solar panels, knowing this was good work, I was happy doing it, and I was good at it.

Part 4: Dénouement and the Dog

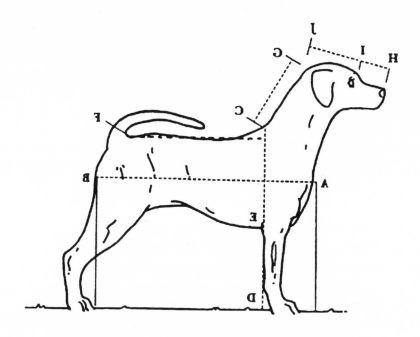

B–A: It felt like the end of the summer, but it wasn't quite.

D–C: We still had a few weeks before I took off for school, a few weeks until Dad would be fully finished with the job of repairing the solar arrays in southwest Kansas.

G–C: One day Rock wasn't on the porch when we came home.

E–D: He was in the ditch just by the road, where sometime earlier that day a truck had hit and shoved him.

E–C: You aren't supposed to go near a dying-but-not-yet-dead dog, but I did. Rock was there, but he wasn't really alive anymore; his coat was matted with blood and dirt.

C–F: The dog died shortly thereafter, and my father silently dug him a shallow grave near the road and then just as quietly went about his evening. It wasn't theatrical remorse, and at the time I wondered why he seemed so emotionless.

H–J: Nearly twenty years later, I'm a father.

I–J: I've buried a dog my son, my wife, and I loved. I spend countless hours staring into a screen, quiet.

I–H: I think I know why he handles loneliness the way he does.

Silhouettes

Roadside Silhouettes

1. I may have understood the power of a bird
2. as an object rather than an animal in flight
3. the first time I killed one.
4. I aimed a pellet gun out a window.
5. I was twenty. All day long I checked corn fields
6. for copper worm populations and mustard weed.
7. Days in the heat, on the ground.
8. I nearly didn't return to school after
   that summer.
9. One night I took my roommate's pellet gun
10. aimed it at a bird on a telephone wire and fired.
11. It never occurred to me I would hit it.
12. And maybe that's why I shot, why a bird's life
13. seemed to mean less to me until I took it.
14. I walked outside to the shared driveway.
15. Nobody had seen what I'd done. I thought
16. I could walk away from an act like this.
17. And while I walked away so many years ago,
18. that bird has flown through so many memories
19. since that summer. Black silhouettes
20. like a flock, or a murmuration,
   or a murder, or a covey.

Fujita Scale

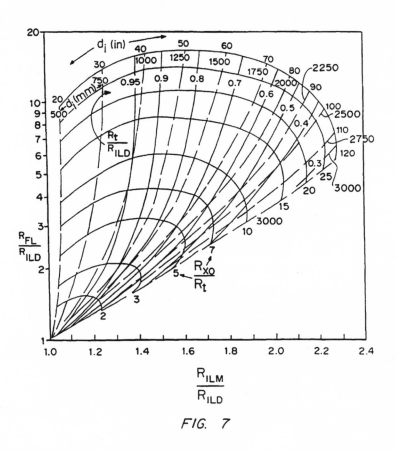

FIG. 7

R_{ILM}: A tornado siren sounds in western Kansas, and we all go outside. I hadn't expected the clouds above to spin so clearly, a mix of black and white paint. At any moment the siphon hose of the sky might appear, dropping like a straw in muddy water. We all felt the air grow lighter.

R_{ILD}: The neighborhood of my youth stood agape at the sky. I knew them all. I hadn't put shoes on, preferring the crisp of grass and then gravel of road pushing against my arches. I took stock of the detritus of life: a privacy fence, a bone-broken garage, our roof, our cars.

R_{FL}: The Fujita Scale comes from the force of a sky wringing itself of pressure. The funnel size or speed of the storm does not matter. We measure a tornado by its damage.

R_{XO}: Once, in high school, we ducked as a class beneath the gymnasium bleachers, jokes flung upward at first. But soon the wind took all other noise away. Even the most foolhardy grew quiet with respect. We took comfort in the collective awe, sunflower faces turned to the air.

R_t: But we did not seek shelter that day, and the tornado did not emerge. The clouds made their slow migration east, and we resumed our lives, neighbors giving a short wave.

d_i: I was the last person standing in the street, feeling gravel beneath my bare toes like a stray penny in a pocket. A loneliness washed over me. If nobody was looking, I might spin into storm.

Prairie Panhandle

Imagine so much state packed into so little space. The prairie panhandles are rectangles of brown grass and wind; even the hard-packed loam is cubed from the shovel. In winter they are merely thresholds in the doorway between states, full of hardscrabble farming and ranching, too little state to shelter against the wind. They have sharp corners, knifepoints, the guerrilla warfare of state boundaries in tall prairie grass. Teeth of barbed wire, a tongue that whistles through the fencing. It is a tightrope of state, and balance is hard. At night on a drive through a panhandle, it is somehow a quieter state. It is the leaky end to the bottle of wine, the final note in the violin trilling and then fading. It is a state of its own, but also somehow a not-state, where the wheels might be off the ground and the hum of the highway disappears in favor of the sound of the state and the state and the state.

The Festive Revolver

....

By afternoon the black powder smoke had crackled and stung the air and idle gunfighters wandered the Front Street replica, a facade of clapboards pasted to the buildings behind them like Halloween masks. There was a dry goods storefront, the Long Branch Saloon, the textile wares. An ice cream parlor. A drugstore. Turn around and there was a parking lot, the contemporary traffic rolling down West Wyatt Earp Boulevard, the hum of midday mixed with the trill of cicadas. Handlebar mustaches and Honda Civics. Dodge City was infused with the scent of the feed yards that circumscribed the city limits. The tourists walked with their children and a handbook to the Old West history of Boot Hill, Front Street, Dodge City. The rough town.

The fast hands of the gunfighters were relaxed as they moseyed down the warped boardwalk, past well-tended grass out front like a gated city park. There was a worn gravel path suggesting a real street, and it faded away into grass at the far end. Barrels and trunks were scattered about the grounds like accidents. A stagecoach and hay cart were parked in front. It was what I imagined an Old West film location must feel like. Cowboys on cell phones, camcorders on the hips of fathers and mothers.

The Long Branch was a real saloon with peanut shells on the floor, beer on tap, a bar filled with chap-wearing outlaws. The mirror behind the bar looked like a holy relic, and the draught handles did not have the names of the beer on them. You stand at this bar, thankyouverymuch, and the dark wood with the dark drapes framing the windows makes you dependent on the sodium vapor light of the antique lamps. They have whiskey on the shelf, but only sarsaparilla on the tables.

Men were armed. I was surprised to see a gun in plain view, easy to grab if I were quick enough. I didn't dare. Like seeing a policeman armed, I was nervous not at the idea of the gun, but at its proximity.

Kids watched the gunfighters from tables, their fathers with them, dressed in shorts and collar polos. Had they seen their own fathers with a gun? Had they been given a toy gun for a birthday? I'm convinced I could tell the difference between a child that has been exposed to guns before and one that has not, but at that moment I was not sure. The next stop for them would be the Front Street Museum, where Bat Masterson's Colt .45 is on display, and then the ice cream parlor.

. . .

We tore down my father's walnut gun cabinet for the dark squares on the chess desk. The desk came from a doctor's office—solid oak legs and supports, cast iron caps, the top destroyed when the office was vacated. The light squares were oak drawer faces from another unfinished desk. The ranks and files were bordered with two-inch planks of oak, miter cut for angled corners, and the sideboards were long, twelve-inch planks of walnut.

We started with the sides of the gun cabinet's hutch and found long planks that had once encased rifles and shotguns, and so must be at least four feet in length. The backing of the cabinet, veneer over cardboard or pressboard, was of no use. The base was a traditional cabinet, used for the storage of ammunition and for handguns, and the doors were two feet by one foot. The sides of the carcass were a separate entity altogether and yielded fine planks between two and three feet in length.

These are the fine materials.

We carefully removed the finish nails and staples, parted the glue with a fine-bladed screwdriver so no unnecessary indentations were marked in the wood. The tops and bottoms were fine planks. The total take was nearly seven one-foot-wide, one-inch-thick planks of walnut varying from three to six feet in length. More than enough for a chess table.

· · ·

The insult, Barry Metcalf told me in an interview some time ago, is the trigger for the gunfight. He and Allen Bailey, both museum employees, met me for an interview in the Long Branch in full costume. They did not look like movie cowboys, and the weapons they used were slung from their belts at the table.

"It used to be a train robbery with a chase and everything," Barry told me. Over the years it has been easier to orchestrate the gunfight on foot, with people occasionally falling from a passing wagon when they were killed. The fight ranges all along the Front Street replica. Among the members of the gunfights, ranging from fourteen to sixteen participants every year, there are people who are employed full-time by the museum like Barry and Allen, and there are men who work with the Department of Agriculture for the marketing news, refrigerator repairmen, body shop mechanics, men from the sheriff's department, and jailers. Some of their alumni include lawyers, bankers, a Russian translator, and teachers.

To break into this fraternal group there is no tryout. It is an incestuous circle: present participants recommend the new members. Former members are still in touch with one another, judging by how much Barry and Allen knew about them. Most times, this arrangement facilitates a sense of trust and respect, as well as recommending participants that are seen to be proficient at the art of gunplay.

They also inherently understand that they will all try to stay in character during their time on Front Street. A bartender with pomaded hair and a blousy white shirt tended dishes behind the bar, and I could hear boot heels on the boardwalk. Barry kept the heel of his palm on the grip of his gun, like an officer resting his hand on a nightstick.

. . .

July 01, 2013 | By Robert Marin | KWCH 12 Eyewitness News

Two people go to the hospital after a shooting at a convenience store in Dodge City.

The shooting happened just before 1:00 a.m. Monday in the 400 block of E. Wyatt Earp Blvd. Dodge City police chief says some sort of confrontation led to the shooting. A woman was flown to a Wichita hospital, and a man was treated at a Dodge City hospital. The victims, identified as 26-year-old —— and 25-year-old ——, both suffered gunshot wounds to the lower extremities.

. . .

Take off the finish from the walnut and the oak. The walnut had a thin polyurethane coat and was easily sanded down until the fibers of the grain rose to the hand like static electricity. The oak was more stubborn, but mineral spirits and sanding slid the wood soft again. Does the removal of the finish remove the previous purpose? When I rub my hand against the oak, does it want to open? When I thumb the walnut, does it house a trigger?

. . .

The trigger of a handgun is a sliver of metal. A waning gibbous. It looks like an outline of the state of Minnesota. The exploded view of a handgun reduced to its individual pieces could be its own neighborhood. A series of long, forward-leaning streets. Imagine the handgun at rest, all its parts separated and laid flat on fine cloth. No longer carrying the tension of the trigger spring, the bolt return spring, recoil spring, ejector spring, sear spring, hammer spring. So many springs that when they are all relieved of their coil, resting on the fine cloth, the machinery takes a deep breath.

. . .

The new participants must endure a two-week orientation to the scenarios that may come up during the gunfight. The training seems to serve a dual purpose: to choreograph the complicated action scene and also to gauge the endurance of the participants. Some men, Barry told me, with the noise and the action, just don't have the constitution.

As part of the initiation process, the new men must die in at least five performances before they are allowed to fire a gun. Most of the people that die quickly are the bartenders and the shopkeepers. Getting a feel for the free-flowing action of this still-dangerous act is very important. Although the guns are, of course, fake, they still put out a great deal of noise, and there are falls that are choreographed from wagons, into water troughs, and from buildings.

The fight itself, I was told, was based on the same principle every year. The Texas Cattle Men (*cowpunchers*, as they are sometimes referred to) come into town, acting obnoxious, and begin a fight with the Lawmen of Dodge City that results in the gun battle everyone comes to watch. The battle usually begins in the saloon and then spills into Front Street. They use .44 and .36 caliber black powder weapons now, as well as .44 mags, .45 regular, and 12- and 20-gauge black powder shotguns. A part of me understands the numerical designation of the weapons, the ballistic significance. In another part of me it is a diabolical math with no equations. No right answers. No proofs and no formulas. A logarithm pulsing with heat and speed.

. . .

The *Dodge City Times*, week of September 28, 1878, regarding the shooting of Frank Trask, a retired Dodge City Lawman:

The Revolver

The revolver was quite festive in Dodge City last week. The Indian "scare" and bad whiskey did much to throw some of the boys off the track.

Sunday night, at about 10 o'clock, Frank Trask was shot while crossing the railroad track near the tank. The ball entered the left side and crossed the backbone to the right side, the direction of the ball being under both shoulder blades. The wounded man is doing well and will soon recover.

Dan Woodard was arrested, charged with the shooting. A preliminary examination was had before 'Squire Cook and the prisoner held in $500 bail.

It is claimed by Woodard's room mates [*sic*] that he was in bed at the time the shooting took place.

. . .

The table's squares were off. One small miscalculation in cutting the blocks and gaps emerged. We shuffled the blocks like solitaire cards, shaved corners, gradually began to see the perfect parquet surface emerge, the grains all facing the same way.

Each block carried a distinct thickness, the raw board resulting in a cobblestone texture. The seams were brushed over with a filler, and the sanding started. All by hand. The motion became important to me, running the paper down the ranks and files slowly, a high-grit sandpaper to start, a decrease in the grit count as the table leveled. The walnut sanded more slowly than the oak. The light tones in the walnut came out, and the table changed and swirled as the grit grew finer.

In my hair, in my clothes, a fine dust gathered.

. . .

Some insults:

He's as dumb as a bag of hammers.
He's plumb weak north of his ears.
His face looks like a dime's worth of dog meat.
He's about as sharp as a sack of wet squirrels.
He's gotta sneak up on the dipper to get a drink.
He's so ugly, he'd make a train take a dirt road.
He ain't fit to shoot at when you want to unload and clean your gun.

. . .

After the insults and the fistfight spill out into the street, a man dies. A lawman, he's killed after words are exchanged, and then the remaining lawmen come from around the corner to confront the cowpunchers.

The lawmen gun down a man who resists giving up his gun, and the quick exchange leaves the cowpuncher on the ground. The smoke is exaggerated with the black powder loads, and the lawmen and remaining cowpunchers exchange volleys until there are only a few lawmen standing. Barry told me that sometimes the cowpunchers win, but I haven't seen one recorded yet. The entire performance is over in minutes.

I was surprised at how close the crowd was allowed to stand to the action. There were picnic tables and standing room just on the other side of the green. Families had lunches with them. On hot days, there is a tent under which folding chairs are arranged. Just over the facades, one can see the modest Dodge City skyline. In the quiet moments, if the wind isn't blowing, one can hear the traffic on Wyatt Earp Boulevard. A cell phone goes off. This might be a public space, except for the anachronism of cowboy hats and six-shooters.

YouTube boasts several home videos of performances, and as I watched several skirmishes a pattern emerged. Standoff in the streets. Humor to get the conflict started. High body count. Vigilante justice incorporated into the act through a bystander finishing off the final "bad guy."

The idea that there were incredible murder rates in Dodge City in the nineteenth century has been a bit overblown. Some estimates give the average as one murder per year, and recent revisions of the history of Dodge City suggest that the area was policed quite well during this time. Liberal views credit the stringent gun law, the sign "The Carrying of Firearms Strictly Prohibited" posted just inside the borders of the city. The numbers don't always include the number of deaths that resulted from police action during that time.

Contemporary numbers are comparable to this time period. Dodge City, in the last ten years, has averaged 1.3 murders per year, not all with guns. There were two stabbings in 2013, for instance. And only one of those resulted in death.

Dodge City is the city of the festive revolver. A mythology of barely-hung-together justice cultivated by Old West reenactments. The city is eager to participate because the weapons themselves fire no live rounds. The dead rise again to take a bow. They build a new truth with the pieces of history they possess.

I didn't have the opportunity to see a performance when I conducted the interviews. Too late in the day. But the haze of the gunfight from earlier that afternoon still lingered, hovering in the eave's corners. The cowpunchers and lawmen lingered to talk to the crowd. Some showed their guns to interested onlookers. They talked about the period-correct outfits and weapons and insults. A degree of accuracy was important to them, and it seemed they passed this desire to the crowd.

At the end of the day, however, they go back to their jobs. They must take off the bandanas and chaps, the chamois shirts and sweat-crusted hats. They put on blue jeans, T-shirts. They are citizens again. They are teachers again. They are curators. They are volunteer fire fighters. They are police officers. They have phones and cars. They blend back into the twenty-first century. But the costumes hang somewhere, the lawman and the cowpuncher waiting to be reassembled.

. . .

Excerpt from the *Dodge City Times*, week of October 5, 1878, regarding the shooting of Fannie Keenan, stage dancer:

Another Victim

The Pistol Does Its Work

At about half past four o'clock this (Friday) morning, two pistol shots were fired into the building occupied by Dora Hand, alias Fannie Keenan. The person who did the firing stood on horseback at the front door of the little frame south of the railroad track. The house has two rooms, the back room being occupied by Fannie Keenan. A plastered partition wall divides the two rooms. The first shot went through the front door and struck the facing of the partition. The remarkable penetration of a pistol ball was in the second shot. It passed through the door, several thicknesses of bed clothing on the bed in the front room occupied by a female lodger; through the plastered partition wall, and the bed clothing on the second bed, and striking Fannie Keenan on the right side under the arm, killing her instantly. The pistol was of 44 caliber, nearly a half inch ball.

. . .

Hammer pin, sear pin, bolt catch pin, trigger pin, trigger bar pin, grip pin. Firing pin. Firing a gun is the surprise followed by the tension.

. . .

The tung oil went on like warm syrup, and a hand's as good as a brush, so I rolled up my sleeves and smoothed it with finger and palm. I could feel the high spots and low spots. We were not professional woodworkers, though my father has gotten much better in the years since we built that table. From old entertainment centers he built my son's crib. From scraps of redwood, blanket boxes. His father bought the remainder of a lumberyard, and much of that lumber is racked in my father's shop like bowed lines of horizon. He's a master of building from the relics of the past.

The oil is absorbed into the wood like tonic, and this table is thirsty. It is reclaimed, and in being so needs nourishment. From my hand to the wood. No longer any gun cabinet or face boards. Later, I will buy a set of wooden chess pieces that fit the dimensions of the board perfectly. Felt on the bottom will let them brush the board like an ice kiss. Chess is a quiet game. It cultivates quiet. It must have a smooth surface, and the board is where to start. The material from which it is made matters a great deal.

Orientation

You were asked to stand with about two hundred other incoming freshmen in a minor lecture hall at a large university. It was orientation, and your mother was whisked away to the parent presentation, and this was the first time you were alone with the other students. The game was, sit down when the number called out was less than the number of students in your graduating class. The first number was two thousand.

A handful of students sat down. They were from Kansas City and Topeka and Wichita. You were sitting in the front and couldn't help but look back at them, envying their situation. They were sitting now, and the game would continue for some time. One of them, you later remembered, had a Mohawk—the first one you'd ever seen in real life. You'd been to Kansas City a few times, when your father took you to baseball games, and one day you'd met Mike Pagliarulo, and he shook your father's hand, and yours. You slept from Kansas City to your home the entire way with a smile.

When they called fifteen hundred, more students sat down. Many more. They were from the same places but were also from Manhattan and Overland Park and Olathe. They were making the jump by five hundred, and still the number was too high for a large majority of the standing students.

They called one thousand, and then eight hundred, and the students really started dropping. Salina, Hays, Atchison, and McPherson. Lawrence and Dodge City and Garden City and Liberal.

They called out six hundred and five hundred and four hundred, and more kids sat down. El Dorado and Newton, and you lost track because at this point the chattering started. There were only twenty or so kids standing. These were the places your dad took you to work, where you ate in restaurants after the heat of the sun and your body slouched in the booths, sapped of its strength.

Three hundred and two hundred and one hundred, and the rest of them dropped. One student from Concordia that was one hundred on the dot raised his hand to ask if he needed to sit down or not because the number was exact. The leader said do what you'd like and he sat down.

You were there with three other kids, and they dropped when the counting went not by the hundreds but by the single digit countdown. Fifty, forty-nine, forty-eight, and the kid from Saint Francis sat down. Thirty-five, thirty-four, and the kid from Lincoln sat down.

Twenty, nineteen, eighteen. He didn't think he'd have to go this far, the leader of the orientation, and he seemed annoyed, like he thought you were lying, but it was just you and someone else in the back, a girl you knew from Utica just a few miles up the road.

Seventeen, sixteen, fifteen, and he was exaggerating, his voice emphasizing the first syllable, his head punching forward for emphasis, and he didn't know when to slow down, and when he said fourteen you sat and the room clapped. Like you'd finished the two-mile race last, but at least you finished. A courtesy clap.

And there was the girl. You might be the only one that knew she'd still be there, that she was going to have to stay standing the entire time.

Five—she was from a school that was supposed to consolidate with your school, being in your vacant county in western Kansas. Parents in the town, however, pooled their money together to keep the school open, defying the state mandates.

Four—she was a track star, and she was on a full ride here, you knew that, because the local paper said so.

Three—you'd seen her at parties, those out-in-the-country parties where the kids started things on fire to keep warm, even if they were things that shouldn't be consumed so easily. She had friends from your school, dated a guy from another high school.

Two—and the attention is so sharp on her that she looks like she might cry. Nobody is talking. This was supposed to be an exercise on how different you all were, how the kinds of people you come in as won't be the same people you leave as. But it became, somehow, humiliating.

One—and she could have found you in the crowd. She knew you, even if you didn't know she'd be at this orientation. But you didn't look toward her, just straight ahead. You waited for the orientation leader, the T-shirt and flip-flops the uniform of the college male you wanted so desperately to wear, to call out zero.

The Flood Plain

1.

The Cimarron riverbed slithers its way through southwest Kansas as the ghost of a river. The sandy riverbed is depressed just deep enough one must have a bridge to cross, but small enough to appear in front of a casual driver as a surprise. Near its entrance to the state of Kansas, the Cimarron National Grassland is home to exotic birds and riparian woodlands. The riverbed is flanked by Chickasaw plum, which are coveted as "sand plums" and used to make preserves and jellies.

Three of us drove to a house just outside of town, our forever-unnamed source for beer, and knocked on the back door. We were not allowed to come out until after dark, and though there were no neighbors, the night was lit enough for us to see the milkweed, thistle, and blue grama growing wild in their yard. I can still smell a metallic residue of combines fresh from cutting back the wheat. In the distance, grain elevators were shining their Texas house lights, open for deposits. It was a Saturday, and the family was watching football in their front room. I imagined there would be any number of illicit things going on, but it was just a family sitting in front of the television, clean and tidy.

They had in their home an industrial refrigerator with glass fronts. Like in a liquor store. The glass fogged when Mr. —— pulled the case of Keystone Light from the cooler, and we gave over the cash. It was fall and cooling down in the evenings, but the fridge looked inviting. We took to the streets instead, a friend behind the wheel, everyone cracking open a can.

I used to think we drank because we were bored. It was a small town after all. But looking back at it, all these years later, I think I'm wrong. When we drove the streets of our small town, we could feel the current of a different life carrying us along. In that short time, we were lucky we didn't die. That might also have been one of the reasons we did it.

We took that beer to a spot north of town, in the country, where a highway crew had parked a front-end loader. We were shielded from the highway by a band of cottonwoods lining the ditch. Every empty can we threw at the machine. The crew had made the mistake of leaving the keys in the ignition, and we drove it around the field in which it was parked. With every drink a new level of destruction occurred to us until lights flashed off the highway and we all scattered, leaving the loader parked, running, the boom of the backhoe lowered to the ground like the tractor was kneeling in supplication.

I still remember the wrongness of it, I mean the way it felt wrong as we did it.

. . .

The Cimarron River is translated as the "Wild" River and was once called Río de los Carneros Cimarrón, or River of the Wild Sheep. More than once it has been referred to by its red color—the Red Fork, Red Salt, Red Clay River. What's in a name? The red color could have come from the clay that slipped into the river in Oklahoma or near the border in Kansas, but it could also be the colloquial name of a river that many of the white explorers, and later white settlers, feared because of their fear of the "wild red Indian."

2.

In 1997 Colorado was ordered to release held water to rivers such as the Cimarron. This flow tore down a great many trees and vegetation that had taken hold in the area, knocking down makeshift bridges with only meager caissons and the smallest gauge culverts.

I imagined that a river began with a rush of water, a head wave, and a whitecap being pushed from top to bottom. I would see it turn the corner, slooshing along the side like a kid screaming down the turn in a waterslide.

The Cimarron River, however, started with only the smallest of trickles, a headstream of only ounces of water. It seemed as though someone had dumped a small bucket of water toward me in the bed. I didn't even know it had turned the corner. I didn't want to touch it for its frailty. In the headwaters a small fish wiggled, what looked to be a rock bass as I would identify it later. It didn't seem possible that enough water existed for it to survive, but it flapped its beige body, struggled, and pulled back to where, apparently, there were deeper waters. I gasped, and as I watched the fish flop and scurry back up the small stream that gathered only the smallest of momentum, I noticed around me other trickles.

The bed transformed itself into a set of channels unlocked. No torrent rushed forth. No frothing white animal turned the corner. Just fingers extending themselves downstream—a constant reaching.

· · ·

The game was simple: toss the empty beer bottles out of the car on the highway and see if we could hit a sign. I was in the back driver's-side seat, so my throws were arched over the car, which was moving sixty miles per hour. I released the bottles very early, and if any made a connection, we didn't hear the crash until we had passed the sign.

In this way we disposed of our childhood.

3.

According to a study by Jeffrey A. VanLooy and Charles W. Martin, published in the Annals of the Association of American Geographers, *the Cimarron riverbed has changed from a wide, braided channel in 1953, when a comprehensive study of the river occurred, to a narrow, meandering channel in 2001, when the researchers retraced the same area from the previous study.*

Legend has it that Jedediah Smith died near the Cimarron River. In many reports of the incident, Smith was killed by Comanche while looking for fresh water.

Smith was known for being a brave "Indian fighter" in a time when many white settlers encroached not only on open ground, but also on native territories. At the time of his death, he worked for the Rocky Mountain Fur Company and was known to make "examples" of Indians he deemed hostile to his company. Yet in these accounts, from other white settlers, he is often found to be dichotomous: reluctant to punish, pleasant to trade with, violent when confronted. He considered Native Americans to be inferior to him, engaging in the all-too-common act of infantilizing those he traded with and encountered.

Smith's body was never found. The group with which he traveled did not stop to track him down when he did not return. By all accounts, the time schedule outweighed the necessity of finding out what had happened to him. His possessions turned up in trade by those who claimed to come by them via Comanche traders. It is after Jedediah Smith we've named wilderness, rivers, trails, and even a Redwood State Park. If the Cimarron River holds any claim to fame, it is as Smith's final resting place.

. . .

Over the next two days as my father and I checked in on it, the Cimarron grew, living up to its name, taking with it trees that had unwisely taken root in the bed. The trees, in turn, destroyed the bridges that had been built over the bed. The water took back what had been its own. My father and I came to visit it over the next week, checking wells in the area and collecting the sandhill plums that my grandmother used to make jelly, and I grew fond of standing with him as I watched a real river flow along its banks. The sand gave off heat like a radiator, but one could feel the cool air when approaching the river. I'd felt that difference when I approached an irrigated field in the summer, or when I peeked over the rail when crossing the Mississippi River for the first time. Mist seemed to float up to me, sprinkle my arms and face, and dry there, cool in its leaving.

Reports surfaced of kayakers, boaters, and canoers testing the strength of the flow. Another man my father worked for took pictures of Mennonite girls, still in full dress and frock, floating down the new river on inner tubes.

It ran, locals told my father, for about two weeks before irrigation tubes began appearing in the creek. Upriver fields needed the water. The river returned to its sandy, dry state.

4.

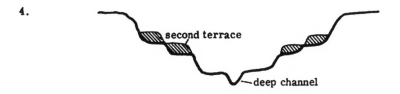

Channel narrowing is in part caused by riparian vegetation; specifically, the production of salt cedar growth has stabilized accumulated silt and sand. This is due in part to persistent drought, irrigation, and an overall decline in the Ogallala Aquifer, and in part to unnatural overall global climate shifts. It is not surprising that salt cedar, a flowering brush, is invasive.

Imagine a landscape one could feel with rough hands. New tactile maps for the blind can give both a relief the fingers can trace and a set of audio links one can access via a special pen that will "read" the more difficultly translated components of the map. Elevations aren't the only spatial components available.

This is to say that maps are primarily visual, and this is their primary limitation. It becomes easy to experience a place as two-dimensional. As flat. As static. But we use another space, a third space, to make the place real. The experience goes deeper, enters the body through a sense of touch.

The river is particularly misrepresented by a traditional map. A tiny blue string coiled across brown plains, green forests, gray mountains. The blue so cerulean it looks as though it is a reflection of the bright warblers that flash across the landscape. That delicate thread betrays rivers that run like stone-color torrents. Like green stale slow flows. Like hidden, underground, secret water.

. . .

David and I drove around town in his cj-5 with a keg in the back from the party the previous evening. We draped an old blanket over it, blue and gray, held in the seat by the lap belt, and drew from it all day. We made sinuous rhythms across the river-streets of that town, going where gravity seemed to take us.

We stopped out of necessity at a park on the south side of town. We got out of the jeep and stretched. We needed to pee. The natural place was down on the riverfront, where nobody would see us.

The river is called Big Creek, but this creek is larger than most rivers in the area. It winds north into the city limits through the park. The embankment is deep, and the roots of trees reach down into the channel like the tendrils of a deep-sea monster. In some cases, these roots are all that keep the rest of the ground from falling into the river.

I took my cup with me down to the riverfront. I'm not sure how I made it down to the bank without falling, but there was no reason that entire day shouldn't have cost me my life. I think about my luck a great deal now that I'm a husband and father. The fall down the embankment would have been the best negative outcome of a day. Every day, I thought, could be as careless as that descent. Every drink a rush like rapids. I wasn't doing anything wrong. As I write this, all I feel is shame for that boy, but there is something that compels me to tell it.

As we relieved ourselves into the creek, a man walked toward us. He was in hip waders, but the water only reached his lower thighs. He trawled the middle of the creek, a walking stick in his hands, poking it into the bed of the creek, a dip and tap from left to right before him. Deliberate, he worked the creek for its secrets. Inside the mesh bag slung over his shoulder were several Frisbees.

A disc golf course ran through the park we'd stopped in, and several of the holes used the creek as a water hazard. Too many players simply gave up entering the creek to retrieve errant discs.

Out of politeness or shame, he tried to avert his gaze. David and I both stopped and zipped up, and David began his stumble up the solid wall of dirt that, in this bend in the creek, rose seven feet high. There were footholds he tried to capture, but he had trouble scrambling to meet them. I could hear him drop his cup onto the silt along the edge of the creek.

But I stayed and watched this man wade the creek. The real world seemed so far above us, far enough away that it didn't seem possible it existed. Even David was gone, and I couldn't be sure he'd wait for me. I felt swallowed by the water, by the channel it had cut out of the ground. I was invincible, I thought. I watched the man meander down the stream, occasionally reaching into the silty bed to pull forth a disc or a piece of trash. It seemed that he might stumble across anything. That there were no limits to the possible disregard the riverbed held.

5.

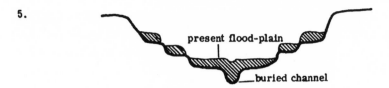

It won't come as a surprise that as the channel narrows and is buried, the Cimarron River's recognizable bed slowly diminishes. There doesn't seem to be an end to this pattern. This will mean more flooding along the floodplain, a more obscured channel, and the eventual loss of the riverbed altogether in Kansas. The Cimarron River will transmogrify into a ghostly remnant of the once sure riverbed.

I've left behind the drinking and the dangerous behavior I was lucky to survive. I can't still believe those days were real. The man who trawled the river gave me the most pitying look, his eyes sad at what had become of me, even though he didn't know where I'd started. He was like a lonely ghost walking through the moment of my life during which rivers crossed. One river's bed contained all I'd destroyed, another picked clean if I were able to take it slow.

I finished out the day with David, but we'd been carried off in the world's sobering afternoon, and soon I found myself dropped at my apartment. I fell asleep as all the invincibility drained from my arms and legs. When I woke it was already night, and I didn't know how the day had floated away. I imagined this was what it was like to be left in a floodplain after the waters receded. I'd planned to get up and go back out, to the bars maybe, look for David again. But all I felt was sadness and that feeling of being lost that comes over every kid in their early twenties. What more could I do? How many more times might I be luckily saved from myself?

· · ·

The part of the Cimarron River that my father and I witnessed running for the first time in a generation has a buried channel. Its floodplain has covered the real water running beneath the surface. It tunnels through the area, growing cottonwoods like eyelashes along its waterline.

If memories are grooves made in the brain, then following those memories is like walking dry creek beds with water at one's heels. When the floodwaters recede they leave a memory groove, a silty evidence of their power. The older a floodplain gets, the deeper those channel grooves.

I didn't notice it when the bed was dry, but when the waters began trickling down in the sand, like they were rising from nowhere, I could see the outer edges of the floodplain. It is a region far more enveloping than I expected, and I had the wherewithal to imagine the Cimarron flooding long ago, spreading its water past its shoulders, like hands holding a cape. The floodplain contains the torrent, a safety net. When the angry river recedes back to its banks, all we have left of the flood is the dried regret of the floodplain.

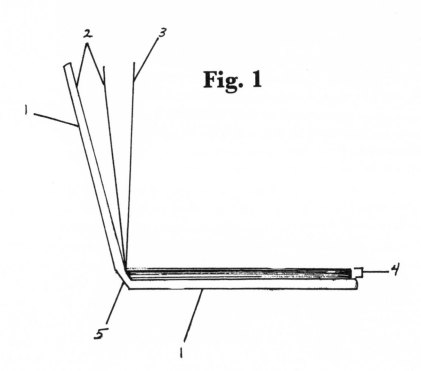

Fig. 1

1. One day, when my father grows too old to work, we will have to tackle the shop.
2. It is a nearly one-thousand-square-foot structure full of the equipment he needs on a regular basis to do his job as a cathodic engineer in the Kansas oil fields.
3. The wind beats against the walls, and currents of air lace the legs of anyone inside. Few windows, but amazingly full of light. There are stations where different kinds of work are done—welding, grinding, cutting and assembling. Many shelving units full of parts he needs routinely in his profession.
4. I assume many sons and daughters my age consider it—how much difficulty there will be in sorting through the belongings of a parent. I think about it a great deal, considering that much of his shop contains parts to a job I don't know, pieces of work-related paraphernalia I don't know the value of or the use for.
5. His shop is vast. It contains the equipment and machinery of the oil field he has worked in most all his life. He is also an avid woodworker, and though I know the basics, there are machines in his shop that mystify me.

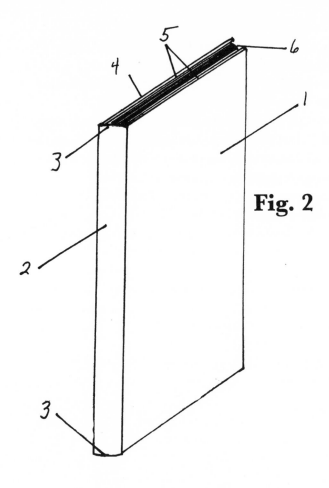

Fig. 2

1. It wouldn't be too much to say that a good deal of his life, were you to distill it down, is in that shop. Certainly some of the most expensive things he owns are there—an arc welder, a beautiful table saw I covet on the regular, his front-end loader, a '78 Corvette and a '56 Willys Jeep in various stages of disassembly.
2. Items with a story, like the lumber he has racked in the back of his shop—wood his father gave to him little by little after liquidating a lumberyard in his hometown. My dad often wondered why he was the recipient of these pieces until grandpa died.
3. The sign for the first business he started. Tools he bought before his children were born.
4. But among all these various tools and spare parts are the manuals he keeps. Pages and pages of exploded-view repair guides for all manner of machines.
5. They are like phonebooks—thick books of thin paper—but three-ring bound. They have greasy prints all over the hardback covers and scratches along the spines. They may have been in some sort of order years ago, but that no longer applies.
6. If the machines are the embodiment and residue of the experience, the manuals show you how to make sense of the story.

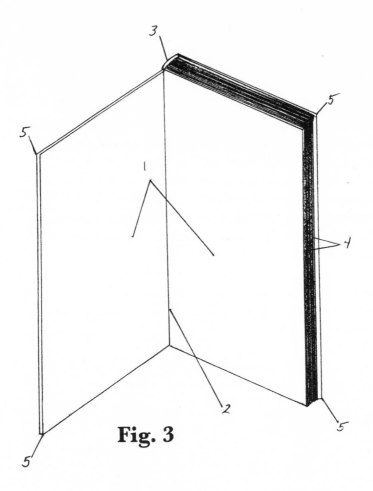

Fig. 3

1. My greatest fear for my father is that he never reaches that age where he is able to retire. My greatest fear is that my time to turn over his shop will be postmortem.

2. Those exploded-view diagrams in his manuals almost don't seem real to me. It is like the seedy back alley of photography where old stuff gets thrown out and picked apart. I pick through the trash. It is like a shop with so many things in it that I don't have the words for. Like my dad's shop.

3. Language can stick with us, but an image can be burned in our brain. An image can be a trigger.

4. How, I ask myself now, might I respond to those volumes of machine diagrams in my father's shop after he has passed? The question can hardly pass beyond my deep interior to land on this page. He is in good health, still working. But I can tell you the conversation between myself and those images will be different.

5. I might look inside those cold machines on the page, past their metal skin and into their meshing gear organs, and see him again.

Stories I've Been Told

Mousetrap

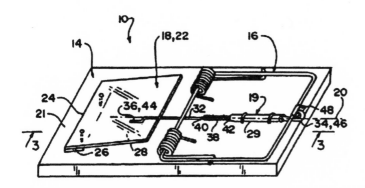

3. My new wife sends me out for mousetraps and peanut butter, and I
   don't think there is anyone that doesn't know what we're doing.

10. Just to throw off the scent, I also grab ice cream and a pack of
    condoms.

14. The narrative of the contents seems to go: traps, sex, ice cream.

16. The traps were once tidy things, flat and discreet.

18. But they don't snap now like they once did.

19. That snap clapped the world shut, a chime in high wind.

20. I've felt that anxiety, like pottery slapping the ceramic tile, but that's
    gone now.

21. Now there are two live traps in my basket.

22. In order for the live trap to work, one must check it often, and we are all full of the sin of neglect.
24. I've traded a fast death for a slow one then, and the narrative is now: traps, sex, ice cream, slow death.
26. I can see it in the cashier's pockmarked face: she sees stories like this one every day.
28. She sees the mousetrap, ones like there once were, perhaps, in her dreams.
29. And maybe the ice cream is slow churn, the peanut butter cheap.
32. The traps slow down in her dream, easing themselves upon the mice.
34. Maybe the mice don't come in at all, but nest in the leftover leaves, swirled crimson in the corner of the yard.
36. The snow never comes.
38. There is never a need for hoarding.
40. Either way, I think she knows what the condoms mean. She probably scans them night after night after work as she sleeps.
42. The narrative always ends sex.
44. I'm embarrassed now, standing there as she slowly bags the items.
46. And there is a whir from the air conditioners, the swish of the automatic doors opening.
48. And beneath it all a noise I can't place, like a scurry in the walls.

Fruit Fly Extermination

....

She's been collecting jam jars and jelly jars and jars that you don't remember the contents of but were probably curry sauces or pickles or something suggested by the shape of the glass to be a one-time purchase. But the memory is gone, and in its place are the fruit flies, many of them, in the summer, in the heat gathered at the sink, latched on to the surfaces and into the drain. She took a sheet of paper and pulled the two bottom ends together and a cone emerged in her hands like a tornado from the sky. Just that suddenly. At its point she left a hole so small only a fruit fly could enter. She placed that in the mouth of the jar, taped the cone to the jar after placing a bit of fruit and some vinegar in the bottom. It seems like she should be interested in what happened next, but she wasn't. Flies came. By the afternoon there were more than one could have reasonably thought were in the entirety of the house. The flies circle the opening, hovering for a moment before settling in to land and then they do a curious thing—they crawl in. They crawl into the opening, pulling themselves upside down into the cone, the hole they enter they'll never be able to find again. Then, one must expect, comes the ecstasy. The jar is amber colored, a disco ball of insects making laps on the dance floor to the apple vinegar and the now-rotting peach. This is the ripe fruit of oblivion: an odor so thick and controlling the fruit fly forgoes its life to stay. Too many fly in the thick fruit air finding no purchase, succumbing to the shortness of their lives. By afternoon, the jar has its population. The summer is like that, a jar of warmth and sweet smells. Lost in thought until sleep takes you. It all starts with the paper tornado and the sweet fruit and the apple vinegar. The warmth of the afternoon and the summer fruit fly lifespan. The jar the shape of some beautiful thing it once held, which it holds, which it will hold again.

Loose Ends

It started with a thread. This was a few years ago, before we'd moved across the thruway from Dunkirk, New York, to Fredonia. The embroidery on my wife's favorite winter coat was unkempt, working loose a glistening tail of gold. It is the thread I always want to pinch between finger and thumb and pull in one tight, suffer-ending yank. But to do this, if the initial solution isn't reached, is to pull more, and I am one that would pull more. I would loosen the fabric and the design in favor of the clean ending to the thread, the satisfying snap it makes, the neat disappearance and tidiness of finality. But to do this to the coat of one's wife is an act of sheer lunacy.

Earlier, the summer after we were married, I'd stopped to show my wife Cawker City, Kansas, and the World's Largest Ball of Twine on the way back from a visit to my parents' house. Squat on the top and bottom, the ball looked like someone had tried flattening it with a spatula. It's a little like I imagined the earth to look after being told in a science class that our world was not a perfect sphere. Inside this ball the size of a massive tractor tire, the likes of which sit on inhuman-sized earthmovers, is one piece of twine. The first. Inside so far, nestled so deep, it never feels the weather change, the light of the sun or the moon.

This ball of twine is in the middle of nowhere, and I've often wondered at the motivation to undertake such a task. I hope it is for the art of it, the beauty of such a thing as a large ball of multicolored twine. I imagine that this is the creative impulse of these people, working with the materials they have like any other artists. The festival that has made this town famous, the Twine-a-thon, might merely be a gathering of artists adding to their triumphant colossus. Yet there was one individual who started with the first thread. That person wound it up tight and waited for the next piece. Then the next. It may not have occurred to them that they were even creating a piece of folk art. They may still not even know what it means to be "folk." They know their world, and they have something that helps them understand it a little better.

My wife took pictures and looked at the town. There isn't much there, but what they have has pictures of balls of twine on it. T-shirts for sale in the post office. A painted piece of twine that leads the curious on a walking tour of the town that might take no more than ten merciful minutes. Plaques and monuments to the ball of twine, referencing of course the old bitter rival ball in Minnesota. She toured all of these with our miniature long-haired dachshund in tow, grateful for the time outside the car.

My first instinct was to pull on the twine, to see the whole ball come apart one thread at a time. Perhaps not a good first inclination when presented with a piece of art, I wanted to see each and every piece of it. To pull that string would be to take it apart, to understand its constituent parts, and as I grew closer to the center I would grow closer as well to history, to understanding, and to the artists. I could see the first thread, and that would tell me so much that I wanted to know about them. It had, however, no real end point. I could find no small tail untucked, no dangling curiosity. All the ends were properly knotted. All the frays tied off.

My wife caught me pulling the thread on her coat. Of course she did. I'm not a man who suffers such temptations easily or in stealth. This was in our old house, my wife's before we married, where we would live for our first three and a half years together. It was a two-story A-frame that found us flanked by geriatric meth dealers and a lone member of a professional barbershop quartet enduring a divorce. I'd poked a hole in the bladder of our aboveground pool the summer before, and the whole sad mess lay exhausted in our backyard, half covered in snow like a fresh mastodon carcass. I had a fence built so the aged meth dealer would stop staring at us as we drank coffee in our backyard in the mornings. Winter is already a cold burden, but so much was unraveling around us in that house that we knew we were leaving despite all the wonderful material I gleaned for my essays.

I found the coat in the dining room and was on my way to hang it up when I spotted it. The thread. The yellow brick road. A miniature dachshund circled my feet, and of course not being my dog but instead my wife's, she in no way warned me that her master approached from the other room.

After the obligatory scolding about pulling a thread in embroidery, she asked me what I thought pulling it would do. "Don't you know the whole thing will come apart?" she asked.

"Of course I did," I answered.

"Then why," she asked. Why pull apart the lovely golden bird on her plum coat? The dog, of course, wanted to know as well, up on her hind legs pawing my blue jeans, thinking I might put the coat on and take her out.

My answer was less than extraordinary. I simply thought I might be able to snap it off quickly and thus eliminate the fray. I told her something to this effect, and she took the coat from me and went to find a pair of sharp scissors.

Resisting the urge to pull at it and take it away, my wife instead knotted the short golden string, ensuring it would loosen no more, and then clipped the dangling remainder away.

The following summer we left Dunkirk for a nice little neighborhood closer to the university, where students shout on the main street just a block from our windows. They are like a plague of locusts, but their path does not quite reach our front door. The house is newer, a tight little center. No meth. No barbershop quartets. I insisted when we looked at houses that there be no pool, aboveground or otherwise. I'm not even sure where the coat is. In our backyard under a small grove of ornamental maples there is a small memorial to the miniature dachshund. My son visits it daily, bringing flowers from our garden. We have a garden. And in that garden all the weeds a man can pull.

Spoor

It is a cold night and we have just received a new dusting of powder. If cold and sunlight are antithetical, as my extremities tell me they are, then cold and night are engaged in a lovely affair.

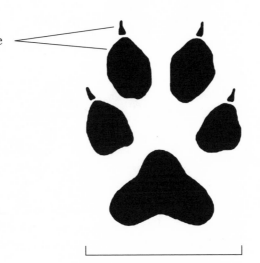

I take my dog on a walk, and he is ill-prepared for the ice and he slips.

The old snow is covered by the new, and so the ghosts of animal tracks dart away from us at all angles. There are three sets of deer prints near the church, in the middle of this town.

All of these animals crossing paths, as their tracks say they do, but they are ghosts too. Deer cross rabbits.

6 to 20 inches

Canine crosses raccoon. The squirrels tumble across our yard, the only disturbance to new snow, and then suddenly disappear as if lifted by a tree limb.

God knows what made the tracks along our back fence line. My wife says peacock and I roll my eyes, but I confess I don't have a better answer.

The dog prances to examine the paths of flight, which will soon be lost to the new snow. Then we turn the corner of the church, a dark south end closest to the empty field where they are known to live, and I see a family of deer. They are fast as impala, fast as antelope. Snow flies behind them.

Let it be a peacock.

Let the unknown world create its mystery prints for us to track. Let there be wild turkey picking at our azaleas.

The deer celebrating their own feast of the epiphany.

There, is that a slither of snake along our unshoveled drive?
The wind creating its own tracks?

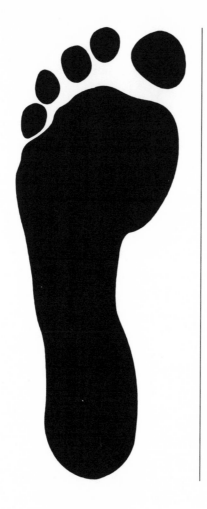

I did not know until later that tracking might be one of the oldest ecological sciences. The spoor an animal leaves behind is its whole travel. The print and scat and broken twigs tell a story of voyages great and small. They leave these books for us. And like good mammals, we try to tell the stories again and again. For that night, let those prints betray the peacock, a vision of teal in snow-covered yards.

Mulberries

I discovered only later that a white mulberry tree launches its pollen at half the speed of sound. My grandfather pushed mulberry branches back and forth with a broom handle to let the light, sweet fruit fall for my wife and me to collect. My wife's allergies are at their peak in the August heat, so she sneezed repeatedly while my grandfather roamed the grass and passed by the bachelor buttons and the wild carrot and the lacy overgrown beauty of my grandmother's garden from which this mulberry tree sprung, of an Asian origin, I would find out later, while he, my grandfather, full-on long-sleeves and jeans even as the temperature approached one hundred degrees, barely broke a sweat. My wife and I, cowering in the shade of the back porch, would run out to collect the fallen fruit, place it in a Tupperware container. The fruit wouldn't make it out of town before we'd eaten it all, and the temperature wouldn't break the entire time we spent in Kansas, and my boys wouldn't even wear shirts some days, and my grandfather only had a few years left on him before a stroke combined with cancer to finally take his life, but before all that he still picked us more mulberries to send us on our way back to New York, a long drive. We ate much more carefully the remaining mulberries, the white fuzzy fruit now cold because we put it on ice, and a handful would be just a little sweet, like watered-down fruit juice, and then the next would rush my senses, a sour so fingertip combined with a sweet so palm that I salivated after the bite, wanting to lick my hand for what was left, but the sensation vanished like a jet leaving a white streak of wash against the sky.

from *Stories I've Been Told*

When I asked my father and grandmother to tell me a story, they told me this one:

My uncle Mickey picked up a hitchhiker in Phillipsburg, Kansas. He died in the car. The hitchhiker. Mickey picked him up walking out of a store, in Phillipsburg, a twenty-mile walk from his home. He walked it all the time, and in the cold or rain sometimes a kind person would stop to pick him up.

The guy's name was Toad Leak, and when I asked, nobody could tell me if Toad was a nickname. He walked to and from Phillipsburg because he couldn't drive. He was dirty, and they thought he'd been abused when he was younger. He was living in what amounted to a shack with a hot plate and no heat.

Homeless, we'd call them now, my dad said. But they found little spots to squat and everyone left them alone.

Nearby Logan wasn't a place where men went without shelter. If they couldn't find a spare shed on a property in or around town, they ventured farther out, for a barn or stable or abandoned toolshed on a farm property. And this was the forties, so there were a number of recently abandoned structures on farmland.

Mickey might have been driving back and forth for a job at the time, my grandmother told me, and so would have made the trip regularly. It is a backroads drive to be sure, and seventy years ago one can only imagine how much more difficult it might have been. Mickey and his wife, Boo, were living in the area for a time before they left first for Pennsylvania, then for Florida.

Toad died just after entering the car. He sighed heavily as he settled himself, closed his eyes, and passed on. Mickey hadn't even made it out of the town limits when he discovered that Toad would not be coming back.

Mickey drove the expired Toad to the hospital, where a nurse came out to the car, pronounced him dead, and directed Mickey to drive him across town to the morgue. He had to put a hand on Toad's chest, my father told me, because there were no seat belts back then, and Toad's head kept hitting the dash.

Of course, my grandmother said, Boo made Mickey sell the car.

My father and grandmother told me this story on the day I arrived after my grandfather died. I'd missed the burial because I couldn't make arrangements to be there fast enough. The extended family had departed.

There were flowers all around, and the house was quiet after they finished telling the story. I was sitting where my grandfather used to sit at dinner, thinking about holding a man up with my arm as we made our way to rest.

The Owl in Twenty-Six Folds

....

10' paper makes a 2.5' tall owl.   Begin white side up.

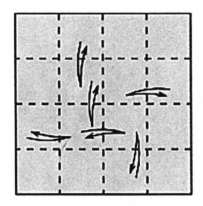

1. It is no accident that the return of the snowy owl to western New York state coincided with one of the worst winters in forty years.

2. The young snowy owl has black barring on his wings, the elderly a ghostly pure white. In the extreme cold they conserve heat by tucking themselves into their layers of feathers, shielding from the wind.

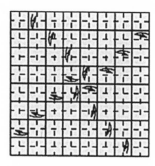

3. Airports from Buffalo to Rochester recorded in excess of one hundred inches of snow for the winter of 2014–2015.

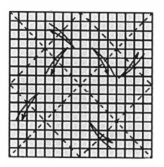

4. The nights became a sanctuary for people here.

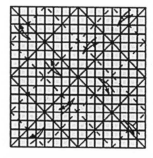

5. The snowy owl perches in the open space for hunting, exempt from the burdens of gravity, where one flicker of prey is in sharp relief to the bone-color tundra background.

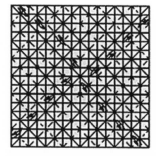

6. Snowy owls frequent the airports hunting voles and other small rodents, but even geese and ducks can be victims of the hunt. The owls are territorial, hungry hunters.

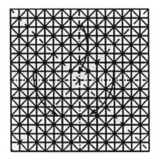

7. The owl is a handy metaphor for survival in the cold night.

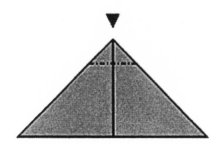

8. My wife and I are night owls in our writing, but on those cold nights we scurried to bed, under mounds of blankets, never wanting to leave.

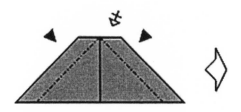

9. The snowy owl's guttural hoots are their love cries. A friend described it as a cold romance, coupling in the chill of midwinter.

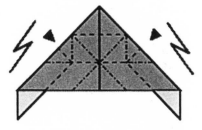

10. The territorial duets are winter song. They skip across the tundra for miles, a guttural bark.

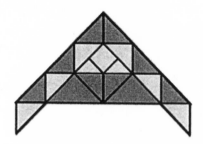

11. When mating, the male presents prey
    with a come-hither beckon of wings.
    And there is a dance of winged rising,
    the prey in his bill. Then the falling
    like a bow, before presentation.

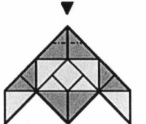

12. Their pellets tell of their desires,
    not the fur and the bone and the
    clingy grass therein, but only the
    meat. They bring the rest forward
    like a crushed Chrysler in the neat
    economy only nature knows.

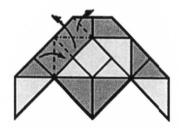

13. And the owl works the night shift.
    At home in the day, roosting, the
    male and female share the duties of
    the nest when egged, and at night
    hunt with those eyes that shine.

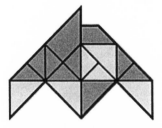

14. Perhaps it is their brooding style,
    their patience, their wide, glowing
    orbs that don't seem flappable
    when confronted.

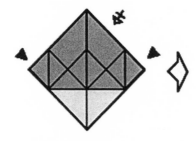 

15. The short days of winter keep the world from thawing. February's average temperature was just above ten degrees.

16. The dramatic ears of some species are just feathers, false ears, a feather hand cupped to the intricate bones and membranes of the canal.

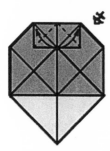 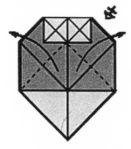

17. Hypothermia occurs when a person's body heat falls below ninety-five degrees. The trauma the body must endure—how precarious our limits in temperature.

18. It was Glaucus the owl who accompanied Athena and so earned his reputation as a bird of wisdom. A bird that flies with the goddess is a bird that has its pick of attributes. The owl has chosen wisely.

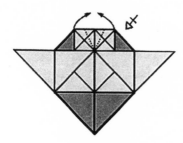

19. The symptoms of seasonal affective disorder include low energy, depression, difficulty concentrating, and thoughts of death.

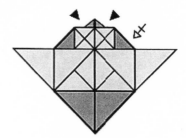

20. The owl's consorts enlivened the Greeks, and the auspices tuned themselves often to the flights of owls. They foretold the weather, the turn of season.

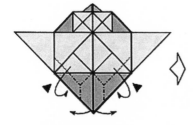

21. Placing a single owl feather near the head of a sleeping human can make them reveal their secrets.

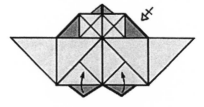

22. In England, an owl nailed to the door warded off evil spirits.

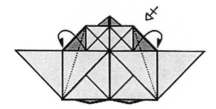

23. In Rome, the call of the common owl was feared, for it was a harbinger of death.

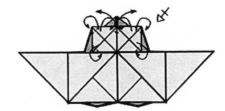

24. Some nights that winter I stared out into the snow and darkness, wondering if anything could live there. My eyes widened, took in what little light reflected off the snow. How can something live in such bitter cold and darkness?

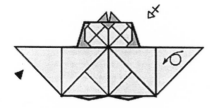

25. The story goes that the everything-maker gave the owl wisdom at the same time he gave it "ears" with which to hear everything, eyes big enough to take in the night, and a neck short so as to support its head.

26. Now, the owl hunts at night, in the cold, against the light of the moon, wisely afraid of the maker.

Jackfruit

Great jade brain of the jungle dropping the branch. The Indians in Kochi warned me not to walk beneath the jackfruit tree for fear of death by gravity. Most jackfruit grew close to the trunk, lesions twirling about under a gaping canopy, but a few bulged from outstretched branches. In the thick jungle of a backyard in India, a novice might not notice them. They have killed children. Twined in their roots are cobras, in their branches a thick, hearty leaf. The enormity of the fruit! Like pumpkins of the sky, they seem to defy what we understand of flora. Jackfruit dangle like a weld about to melt at the point of contact, and the fruit, like a stack of metal plates at the end of a pumpjack falling when the weld melted one day and crushed a man I knew in the oil field thousands of miles away, and I look at these fruits and consider why I ever thought God was beyond the reach of gravity. Of all the physical laws, the jackfruit tells me, He loved falling best.

The Traffic in Kottayam

The man across the street died on Monday night. The rains hadn't started yet, and so the days in southern India, Kottayam, sweltered. Dampness hung in the air, like little beads of water off a telephone line. The monsoon grew closer and closer, an early arrival for that year. My wife's grandmother kept food on the table almost the entire day, different bowls and plates of food I couldn't keep straight because they shifted so often. Egg curry would come and go, as would olan and avial, bone-in chicken curry, spicy fish and soothing yogurt, dosa with sambar, dishes I didn't even have an opportunity to identify. I was sitting at Kochamma's table, reading the paper, when I heard the wailing. The sound of genuine pain has only one tenor. It is deep not in tone but in sorrow. The animals in the yard, the parrot and the goat that my wife's grandmother kept, were silent. There were no crickets in this early morning. I looked out the windows lined with bars to deter thieves, past the mango tree and the red gravel, past the gate and to the opposite side of the street. One of the maids swept the gravel for fallen vegetation, and the slipping sound of straw on pebbles could be heard only when the sister of the man who had died stopped wailing to take another breath.

This was dying in India. The public outcry observed by family and neighbors. I sat trying to read *The Hindu*, the only English-language newspaper we could get in Kochamma's neighborhood. Cabinet meetings and cricket matches. Jewelry thieves and hit-and-run accidents filled the pages. The news there didn't comfort me any more than the news in New York. The bus full of commuters hit head-on was an ongoing investigation story during the time I was there, and the traffic situation in the district was hotly debated.

I was passive, sitting at the table, afraid of this event that began to form. Many people gathered at the house across the street under a makeshift awning hung with rope. They took refuge under trees in Kochamma's yard as well. Many paid respects as they left for work; they waited to listen to part of the mourning song and then made their exit. The men craned their necks to watch whenever they caught a glimpse of me. I wandered the yard looking at the jackfruit tree, tracing the lines of the drive to the street, playing with the parrot in the cage that screamed *thaata may pucha pucha!* (Watch out! There's a cat!). But I also wanted a better vantage point from which to see the wake.

Just the previous night we'd attended an English-speaking Catholic mass. I knew the whole routine, and it was the first time something I truly recognized showed its face. The mass played out with only a few small variations from the ones I'd attended with my mother as a child. In those days I had been disinterested, bored, going through the motions, but now, in the first Catholic mass I'd been to in years, I relished the ceremony. The voices of the thick Indian accents now rarely went misunderstood because I knew the words they would say.

The church was a relic of the Portuguese. The floors were tiled in a rich pearl, the ceilings vaulted with beams of dark wood, the hallmark of this area. Every wood structure and handicraft bore its signature dark, rich wood. The stations were painted on wooden slats that hung from the walls circling the large, open worship area. There the pews divided the congregation by gender, men with dark pants and button-down short-sleeved shirts, their heads bowed in prayer, women in dresses, solemn. Children knelt in the middle, in the aisle. In the whole middle of the church, where one would expect to find more pews, there was nothing. All the pews were as close to the wall as possible, off the smoky tile. There also a monastery provided easy access to the church, and four nuns in full habit in the heat sang all the songs into a microphone. Their high voices rang through the emptiness of the church. They floated out the open doors, down the path, and mixed with the hum of traffic, the beeping horns, boys playing cricket in the fields, women hanging laundry outside. Their voices were like a high-pitched cloud, a puff of smoke with sharp edges.

After a few hours the sorrowful song died down at the neighbor's house. More people arrived, standing in the street. Men brought food for those waiting in the heat to pay respect, and the tent filled with makeshift tables topped with dishes and bowls of all sorts. Jimmy Uncle, the driver, took us into Kottayam, the city, to pick up some things we needed. He opened the gate while we piled into the small car, and beeped a few times to get the congregation to move slightly, and again to alert oncoming traffic. Driving, or rather being a passenger in a vehicle in India, is difficult. There are few observed traffic rules similar to ours, and after the first few narrow misses I resolved to just accept that my fate lay in the hands of the oncoming traffic, and trust that somehow I'd make it through.

Honking became a language. As Jimmy Uncle passed slower traffic, veering into the oncoming lane (the right side of the road rather than the left), many times there would be a bus bearing down on us, honking not out of impropriety, but to help communicate. Jimmy Uncle honked back, to warn the car he was passing that he would be returning to the lane, and the driver gave him just enough space to do so, while the bus passed us close enough that I could touch it. Not that I would; my wife said many times to keep all limbs in the vehicle for fear that I might one minute have a right arm, then next pull back a bloody stump.

The streets veered uncontrollably into one another. Men lined the street and held their *dhoti* with one hand to let some air enter on their legs, the women flipping the end of their sari over their shoulder. Many walked in the street on the occasion that a sidewalk was not available. At times, when we would visit the money-exchange office, or when we went to the *DC Bookstore*, the constant turns and downhill gait felt like we were traveling down an apple peel, and I wondered when we would find the end of the skin. We were like the penny that is tossed into the funnel, circling with more and more momentum until it can no longer sustain itself and flattens out. Motorized rickshaws weaving in and out of traffic even on these side streets, small junk cars passing BMWs. The traffic was always relentless but always moving.

The night after the final song rang out from the neighbor's home, the monsoon rains started. Harsh, angry torrents that bored grooves into the drive, slapped the roof, and stopped as suddenly as it started. Everyone took shelter. The mourners had dissolved into the steam of the day, as had their song. The afternoon held a wet rag to my mouth. I was still a stranger. I followed the story of the bus as long as I could, but it seemed there would be no resolution to the case. The responsible parties were killed, the victims nearly forgotten in the news cycle, the survivors of those victims in their own mourning, singing their own songs. Kochamma left the midday snack on the table, and from the dining room a new song, her voice calling out, *Eat. Eat. I made this for you.*

Take an Island, Give an Island Back

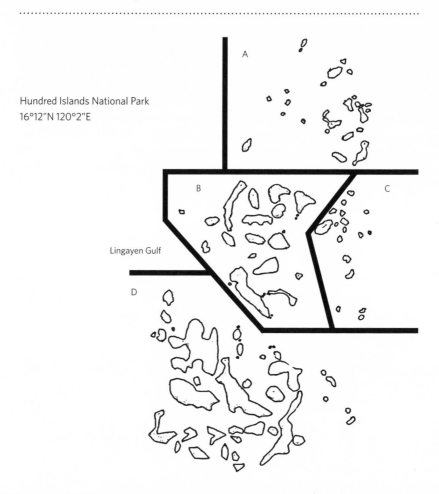

Hundred Islands National Park
16°12"N 120°2"E

Lingayen Gulf

A

B

C

D

A.

1. The Lingayen Gulf cups these islands like marbles, their green swirl of vegetation like frosting on a cupcake, their pronounced tufts like hairy moles, polyps.

2. From the sky, Braille. From the water, a cityscape.

3. In the night, the count becomes 123 or 124 islands depending on the tide.

4. The tide takes an island, the tide gives an island back.

5. And there is my wife, whose belly is an island with a lone inhabitant.

6. He has raked his foot across the island like kicking off a night blanket, like I do in the heat of the Philippines.

7. Pangasinan Province in the north is far from Manila, far from the military and the crowds, the jeepneys jeering down the streets.

B.

1. We stop at Quezon Island, a beach and resort stop, for lunch. It is one of the larger islands, on the outermost chain, a forty-minute trawl.

2. We disembark, shoot photos of the rainbow pontoons docked along the port, the children playing in the water, following a pale fat man with an enormous white beard, calling after him *Santa Claus, Santa Claus!*

3. He responds not unplayfully, by splashing them with water and smiling.

4. My wife, worn down by the trip, sits beneath the cover of the open-air restaurant, urging me to go explore.

5. Her mother will take care of her, she says. The wait staff is attentive, and she already has water and food, so I walk down to the beach.

6. To the north of the restaurant, near the shade the trees of the island provide, there is a floating dock a few feet out, a line of timber leading to it.

7. I've removed my shoes and socks, cuffed my shorts high, and I begin to ease my way to the planks.
8. Beneath me, the shallows are littered with the capiz shells that many of the locals make a living harvesting from these waters.
9. I'm surprised to find them, little glitter fins in the sun.
10. As far as the eye can see there is no open water but just islands, stepping stones. Pregnant bursts of green in the blue water.

C.

1. I think about living on one of these islands. Isolation in a landscape the size of a house in New York state.
2. A boat docked at a reasonable inlet where the water rises to the surface of the ground.
3. Just us and a son.
4. He is already island people.
5. I look over at my wife and find her eating and talking with her mother, both of their profiles toward me, looking out at the beach with the old, pale man walking away from the screaming kids, the Marco-Polo call of *Santa Claus* reaching me still.

D.

1. In the night, later, when we are in bed and I feel my son kick again and again, the tide recedes and deposits another island in the archipelago.
2. I imagine its tales of travel are incredible, submersed in the new world of ocean.
3. I imagine all the other islands leaning in, drawn to the story,
4. listening carefully to its water birth.

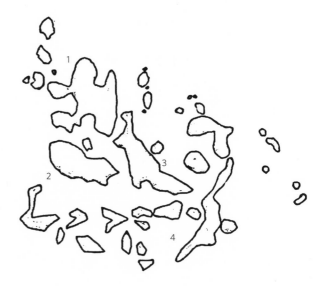

Missing Person

I was not the first person to venture into the woods looking for the boy, but I'm the only one who went in that far. The square mile of undeveloped ground was surrounded on all four sides by houses, backyards butted up against heavy thickets of lilac, juneberry, and dogwood threaded with ivy and budding winged elm. Inside the territory were forts built by the local kids from fallen branches and a burned-out Mazda thoroughly abused by time and childish aggression. Dry elevations that winded themselves through the expanse like a mad dike, and low points holding on to the week's rain. Poison ivy painted the areas around brush and thicket. There was spotty sun puncturing the canopy, and the sound of light traffic in the streets and jays scaring off other birds. A dog barking. I was surrounded and alone.

The boy was nowhere to be found. I could hear his name ring through the streets just outside my vision. The wild space let that little tinder through. And then I found the fawn in the divot near a volunteer elm deep in the expanse. It was curled up so tight one might have confused it for a stone. White spots traced from its head around the curve of its back and disappeared into the old leaves gathered there from the previous fall. It had tucked its nose under its back leg, no doubt hiding from my clomping feet and voice calling out the young boy's name.

I stood there for a moment. I'd been slogging through brush and along small creeks, through backyards and up and down neighborhoods, calling this boy's name for hours, and a ghostly echo of his name tapped back at the foliage. The quiet of the woods and the miracle of the animal hushed me. It felt like being in blanket forts as a kid when my parents were in the room talking. There but not there. Maybe I'd disappear too if I were that kid and my mother said to me what she'd said to him.

A cop stumbled into the brush after a short time, and I stepped toward him, past the fawn. He asked me if the bike he'd found there was mine, and I told him it was. Yes, I was looking for the boy. No, there was nothing here. I didn't turn around, but instead walked the officer out of the thicket, away from the fawn, into the boy's name swimming the streets.

from *Stories I've Been Told*

··

When I asked a student to tell me a story, she told me this one:

When she was little, her father told her he once watched a house burn down in the middle of the night when he was a young boy. He and his brother, her uncle, were not asleep as they should have been, and they spotted the glow of the fire. From their window, they watched across the street as the fire broke out the windows, started to come outside from the inside, and burned all night. Help arrived too late to save the house.

When I imagined this, I imagined their chins on the sill, noses pressed to the glass. I imagined pajamas with buttons, like none I'd ever had, but what I'd imagined a generation previous to me wore.

When I asked her whether he had told anyone that there was a fire, she told me she hadn't thought to ask. She'd always been interested in the sight of him watching the fire burn.

When I asked if he remembered anyone dying, she said he hadn't told her that either.

When I asked, What did he tell you about the fire?, she said he told her about his fear. She told me that he and his brother couldn't sleep that night when the fire started, and when the fire trucks finally came, after the fire had done its work, he hadn't known so much time had passed, that the night had seemed to evaporate.

When I recalled them, these weren't her exact words. They are what I remember of the story, told to me many years ago in an office littered with paper from desk to floor. She was struggling for a good story because the stories she wrote felt like staring into a pitch-black night, told there was a rendezvous in the distance but hearing only a muffled embrace.

When she talked, she fiddled with her thumbs.

When I told her this was a story to tell, she smiled. She was a timid student, and I often worried that I made her nervous in class because I might arbitrarily call on her for an answer or a snippet of her prose from an exercise. You can tell it, she said. I could never tell it.

When I asked her why, she told me it was about her father. She offered no further explanation, and I sought nothing further out from her in its regard.

When she left the office, I jotted the story down quickly in a notebook where it remained for years. What I found out between then and now was that wild fire started 420 million years ago, increasing as oxygen and vegetation took hold. We controlled it about 1 million years ago. We generated food and protection. We burned cities and villages and have seen forests leveled in its path. We developed it for propulsion nearly 200 years ago. We discovered plasma 130 years ago. Some fire is courageous, roiling forth, and some fire is cowardly, smoldering. I've seen a father, whose child died in a fire, in line near me at the grocery, and perhaps I imagined it, but he seemed to still give off heat. Fire can burn on water, in the air, just before one's eyes.

When I smell fire from chimneys, I remember first the smell of a burning cornfield in Kansas when I was a child, a farmer clearing his stubble, the acid and the smoke choking me. I watched it as my father drove us along the highway, after we were out of range of the smell, a small rooster tail presenting in the distance. I don't remember saying anything, but watching the stem of smoke develop into plumes. Perhaps we forget the fire burns so we can see it. In that way, fire is responsible. Some fire is bright to the eyes and guides us, and some is dim in the distance, a signal beacon losing fuel until it is just a slip of light seen through two windows.

Texts Real and Imagined

from *The Moon Illusion Notebooks*

[Moon Illusion]

The moon appears larger in the sky at the horizon, as an oasis of orange, but it is physically farther away. This is usually earlier in the evening, and as it rises in the sky it diminishes ever so slightly. Perhaps atmospheric refraction combines with the optical illusion of proximity to fool our eyes and senses. We think we understand distance because we have depth perception, but lost in all that space, might anything seem to be drifting away from us?

[to be in syzygy is to be aligned]

The night I met my wife, we parted and then realized the moon was full and red and in eclipse. Apogee, perigee, blush. Always returning. If the supermoon is the moment when the moon is full, new, and at perigee all at once, what astronomers call the perigee-syzygy, then the lunar eclipse is the effaced-syzygy. It is said the syzygy can cause moonquakes. It is said syzygy increases the tides. Alignment can make all manner of things shake.

[A Night in Egypt]

Ptolemy knew the moon could mislead you. From Alexandria he would have nearly felt he could touch it atop the grand library. Dark Egyptian nights when the moon walked with him it felt so present, like a domesticated pet on a starry leash, it interrupted his definition of the forty-eight constellations. No matter. He walked with it anyway, watching it wither as the night passed, the air still warm off the desert sand, his teachers already in bed. As the moon rose, he measured its shrinking, a small white puddle in its zenith.

[Easter Night 2008 pt. 1]

My wife and I go out to find the Paschal Full Moon, coats and hats, the wireless monitor slipped onto my shirt collar while our son sleeps. Breaths are painful, sorrowful, a taste of dust and moisture, which should be mud but isn't, and we look for the moon along the horizon lines as best we can but find nothing. My son and I were born under the waning gibbous. My wife was born in the waxing gibbous. We circle the moon fed and full. We satellite each other in cold, bright light. Perhaps we are too early for it this evening. Perhaps we will have better luck finding it later in the night, when even the streetlights bow to the lights in the sky. It is Easter night, and there is little movement on the street. Easter is early this year; we've heard everyone talking about it on the radio, but it doesn't strike home until now, the silent evening just for the moon. The snow is gone; the grass is exposed and not happy about it. I want to say to my wife that it will appear, that this moon is just hiding behind a rooftop that blocks us, but I am not sure myself, and so instead say, "Let's try again later."

[Moon Gardens: A Tour I]

Sweet Alyssum
White Swan Hydrangea
Moonflowers
Iceberg Rose
Playa Blanca Dahlias
White Pearl Hyacinth
Snowdrops
Delphiniums
Lupines
Lamb's Ears
Stainless Daffodil
Bleeding Hearts
Candytuft
Lilies of the Valley
White Snapdragons
Crocus

[Moon Gardens: A Tour II]

I saw a moon garden at a resort we visited right after our son was born. To our left, a sidewalk slid down a hill, and I had the baby in a carrier strapped to my chest, where he peered out with round moon-eyes not settled on their color. People walked the sidewalks in twos and threes. In the distance I could hear the indistinct sounds of a lecture taking place in the outdoor auditorium. The buildings around us no less than eighty years old, tall, and moneyed. We could have been moon garden plants ourselves, looking up at everything we passed, pale in the light of it. Glowing in its wake.

[Naming the Moons: A Guide]

They are round and they are light, and so they must have seemed like they were entities, gods, flashlights with intention, deserving of a moniker that might serve to distinguish that darkest of skies, the one that the full moon makes dark through its radiance. My son's namesake is the Paschal Full Moon, also known as the Egg Moon, the indicator of Easter, even though he wasn't born under this moon, but in the late May Flower Moon instead. His name, Pascal, is French for "spirit of Easter." Tonight he has some trouble going down, but he eventually sleeps for almost twelve hours straight, hours that his mother and I will worry. Then he rises. He is almost one at this time. Depending on the time of year, you can see the Crow Moon, the Harvest Moon, the Pink Moon. There is the full Worm Moon, the Cold Moon. Look around you—what does the moon illuminate? What feelings does the moon raise in you? What moons return for you?

[Lunar Nomenclature]

Giovanni Riccioli knew how to name a moon feature. His *Mare Tranquillitatis*, or Sea of Tranquility, still stands after 360 years. The International Astronomical Union now specifies that any name for a place on the moon must belong to a deceased scientist, preferably one that studied the moon in some way. There have been names for astronauts who have perished in the name of exploration as well, and scientists of note who have had little or nothing to do with the moon. This procedure began with Riccioli too, naming smaller craters within his "seas" for respected thinkers of his time. But the early names listed on Riccioli and Francesco Grimaldi's map from *New Almagest*, names that would describe large tracts of the moon's visible surface, used the artful names for weather, such as *Oceanus Procellarum* (ocean of storms) and *Mare Nubium* (sea of clouds) and *Insula Ventorum* (island of winds). What these two Jesuits saw through their telescopes in 1651 was a vast ocean of space they imagined ebbed and flowed with activity.

[Easter Night 2008 pt. 2]

Later, when my wife comes downstairs and wants to have another go at seeing the Paschal Moon, I walk back out and finally feel the light of the moon. That light at night is heavy, like high humidity for the eyes. The light is unnatural, and so the things it exposes—animals that usually creep about unseen, or the soft fence line of my neighbor's yard, where the taller decorative grasses sway in a night breeze—are imbued with solar echo; they are lighted, but are not the items they are supposed to be. I see a scraggly cat poke its head from the culvert in our neighbor's yard, white and glowing. My wife's back is to it, and she, coatless, only out to see the moon for a couple of seconds, does not see this glow. Again, we are all one moon garden come to life, even my son in his crib upstairs, his window taking in the glow as I know it must. All of us move in new orbits: the cat, my wife, our son. We are all of us pale and pulsing beneath this moon.

Drop Off

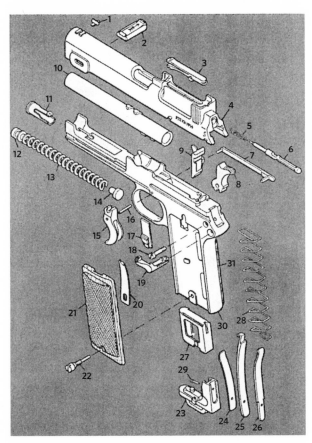

(1) I'm not allowed to walk my son to his classroom. (2) In the effort to assert more independence, children (3) negotiate the hallways themselves, (4) sliding their bags and coats into cubbies. (5) Imagine legs like springs (6) sitting too long, (7) tension like (8) a hammer, (9) parents skulking to cars. (10) First grade a barrel (11) negotiating the rifling. (12) I used to guide him (13) through the twisting halls (14) until our memories (15) triggered (16) the same turns. (17) Do they not want us (18) wandering the halls? (19) A plague of parents grasping (20) at any purchase. (21) I am exploding the gun (22) I fear walks in instead of me. (23) I cannot continue a fear of the dark halls I cannot see. (24) When he walks, the sidewalk (25) blows him to the doors. (26) He is small now, (27) he doesn't turn to wave. (28) It is cool for September. (29) What use are the glass doors (30) to his school except to let (31) the light in?

The Graduates of Fly-Fishing School, Sarasota, Florida, Class of July 13, 2013

There were Quaker parrots nesting in the palms off Midnight Pass Road as evening approached. In a repair shop parking lot, twenty tourists watched an experienced fisherman cast a fly back and forth toward the closed garage door, the line whipping in an elegant script *s* elongated to the snap of the rod, then pulled back as if by the tide, a wingspan of forty feet. The fisherman, in shorts and a T-shirt, didn't look the part of the fisherman. The tourists donned fly caps and some wore hip waders, all paying close attention to the stroke of the line. I caught only this glimpse as we drove past, on our way to the beach rental we'd procured for the week. This fisherman casting and pulling, casting and pulling, and a handful of the tourists mimicking the arm motions, so they all looked as though they were throwing fetch. That night a man who killed a teenager was acquitted, and outside the Quaker parrots continued squawking their shrill bleat, their nest enormous for the tree in which it rested. Made by fastidious builders, the nest seemed to almost tip from the tree with a breeze. I could only think about the tourists taunting a line to the birds. The fly hovering before them and then pulled back. My boys in the room, preparing for bed. No doubt the Quaker parrots entered their dreams, cast there by invisible hands.

Exploded View

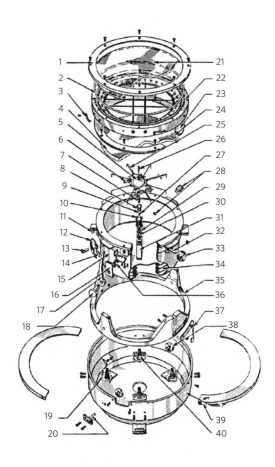

1
2
3
4
5
6
7
8
9
10
11
12
13
14
15
16
17
18
19
20

21
22
23
24
25
26
27
28
29
30
31
32
33
34
35
36
37
38
39
40

1. It's when I get lost,
2. and the best way through
3. is somehow in the details.
4. It happened on a bike one afternoon,
5. neighborhoods gave way to country,
6. and all I could find was graveyards,
7. three country plots down one road,
8. and now the deceased were markers.
9. It was a comfort.
10. I sat on a bench where mourners rested before,
11. and a cross-section of humanity rested with me,
12. an exploded view of the narrow town
13. from which they died away.
14. Lay every dead person head to foot
15. and the distance would extend
16. to any god that has ever been prayed to.
17. Suddenly the compass righted itself in my head,
18. and I found home.
19. Or when my son disappeared one afternoon
20. as I worked the garden.
21. I'd pulled pachysandra and ivy
22. from the beds and foundation of our house,
23. wads of it in my hands,
24. pulling back like I rode a row machine,
25. my back curled and straight.

26. And then he was gone and that street-terror sound
27. of locking brakes is all that can fill your ears.
28. I ran the house twice shouting the boy's name.
29. And then I could see the yard
30. as though it were a machine
31. reduced to its constituent parts.
32. Thickets spread apart and exposed, the air
33. between their branches and the decking inhaled,
34. the spaces parting.
35. Feral can be a temporary condition.
36. I found him in our shed
37. and didn't shout as I might another day.
38. I put the dirt and green detritus of pachysandra in his hair.
39. It was how I could bring him back to me,
40. and put the world back together.

Nesting Box for the Eastern Bluebird: A Guide

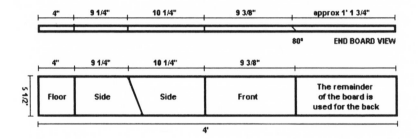

1. Consider the nest box my sons and I assemble from a kit. It is shaped like a rocket, and they paint it in bright colors. The nose cone roof is bright red, the fins blue and white and green—a boxy projectile hovering beneath an ornamental maple in our backyard. We can't open the enclosure once I've sunk the screws in the soft pine, so the birds will be safe. I had never considered that the job of the nest box was safety. Before I'd put screw to wood, I'd thought of nesting boxes as items for study, a display, if you will. In some ways the opposite of safety. But the precision of the hole for the entrance, the way the bottom is clipped so water and filth can escape, even the manner in which it hangs, speaks to safety. The boys run in and out of our house to grab new paintbrushes, more water, a towel to clean up the mess, with the constant *thwack* of the screen door.

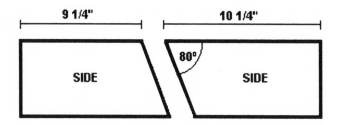

2. The eastern bluebird is a flash of blue on fire. Seeing them in town in western New York is rare, as they tend to populate open areas with short grass. The bluebird is an ardent and caring parent, the male and female sharing "diaper duty" by taking pellets out of the nest constantly, taking turns close to the brood to ward off any predators. Here the birds avoid pesticides, which have crippled their numbers. They fight for their territory endlessly against other bluebirds. When two male bluebirds fight, it looks like drunk wrestling, with wings. They skitter along the ground, occasionally taking to the air, attached often enough. When they separate, they eye each other down and attack again. There is frequent pinning, the beak holding the competitor down.

Bluebirds also fight nonnative bird species such as wrens and house swallows. The house swallow is one of the invasive species not protected by law in the state of New York, and they are a constant menace to bluebirds and to birders alike.

Remove the house swallow nests repeatedly to discourage nesting, the New York State Bluebird Society says.

Deal with them as you see fit.

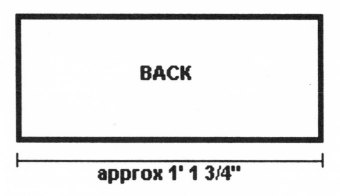

BACK

approx 1' 1 3/4"

3. Fifteenth-century bird enclosures looked like water vessels growing goiter-like from the sides of homes, the mouth open to the world. A small extended lip invited perch, and the narrow neck provided the foyer to an expanded main bedroom. Birdhouse keepers used them to rid themselves of the pests the birds had become to their fruit crops. Some would cover the opening with their palm and shake the house until the bird died. In this way the orchard was saved, but a bird was lost. Many birds were lost this way.

These clay enclosures must have seemed so safe to a bird in the wild at first.

Other birdhouse keepers collected the eggs and baby birds in these clay model homes for food. Dovecotes, the earliest bird enclosures mainly used for pigeons and doves, would lead to the first domesticated food source and would help feed countries like Turkey, Egypt, and the Netherlands during periods of drought.

4. I have lived in apartments and I've lived in rooms. I've lived in A-frames and I've lived in offices. The only thing they all had in common was a bed. Perhaps for me that is the very base definition of a "house." It is my wife and our children that have complicated that definition for me. A bed is no longer enough. I think of a house now as having locks on the doors to protect our young. I think of it as a touchstone. The thought of our house is bound up in the way I think of my wife fashioning mystical gardens of lilies and daffodils. As we build our rocket birdhouse, she is in the dirt, pulling weeds and marking space for new flowers she will propagate herself from cuttings and seed. Our deck is a part of our house. Our yard. It is no longer a structure but an idea of bounds and limits in which we feel safe. She comes to the deck ready to wash the earth from her hands, and compliments the boys on their colors, helps the little one spread the paint rather than glop it on. The little one is all too eager to pull the brush across the wood, and then she is gone inside, having worked her magic on these two paint-spackled chicks.

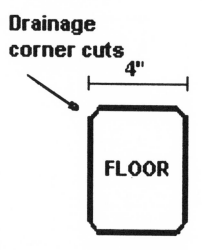

Drainage corner cuts 4"

FLOOR

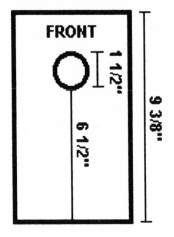

FRONT

1 1/2"

6 1/2"

9 3/8"

5a. The gourd house kept insect-eating species close to Native American communities for some time before Charles Waterton would be credited with ecological birdhouse construction. Waterton would be the first to use the birdhouse to revitalize populations devastated by human interference. He would surround his estate, Walton Hall in Yorkshire, with nine-foot-high walls to create the first known nature preserve for animals and waterfowl.

Where many birdhouses before it were either repositories for food or devices for pest control, the front door of Waterton's birdhouse was cut only wide enough for the bird to enter. A side or top could be removed to clean the enclosure. Gourds and simple entry structures could not be. Gourds blend into natural structures and itinerant communities and are incredibly easy to make. Waterton's nesting boxes mimicked the structures of human enclosures, making them just *beyond* nature.

5b. We built birdhouses out of clay and woodcrete long ago, and they looked like kitchen items. Perhaps it felt like an extension of our pantry. We might be our most animal selves in the kitchen, after all.

When we built them out of wood and gave them roofs and walls, made them look vaguely like our own domiciles, all that changed. They became tiny families instead of a food source. They joined the neighborhood.

I've always thought ecologists and scientists call birdhouses "nesting boxes" to leave out the element of anthropocentricity. When we call something a house, we consider it human. Apart from nature. Nest boxes sound like something we can observe objectively.

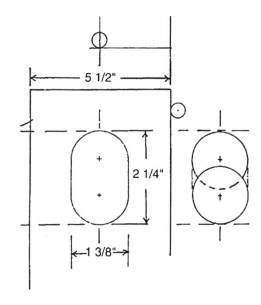

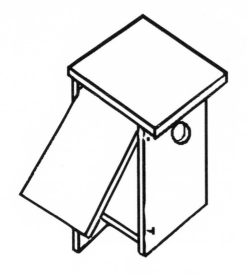

6. It is easy to anthropomorphize birds. Their falling numbers a crisis, a *genocide* according to one bird website. I know of few species that have such dedicated followers as the bluebird. It is true that there are few flashes of blue so startling as the bluebird on the wing. Even the blue jay doesn't compare in brightness. The eastern bluebird has made a resurgence due to the proliferation of free plans online for building your own nest. Landscapes in western New York are dotted with them, like Roman candles ready to fire.

Lay them out of the way of wooded areas to keep them from other invasive birds.

Keep predators away by making it impossible to climb the post upon which the box is mounted.

Do not expect birds the first year.

7. The boys finish painting, and all there is to do is watch it dry. So they get their soccer ball and begin a small game, the older one dominating the field while the younger cries foul and demands the ball. They beg me to play, but I demur. There are times when a moment is too much for me to intrude on, and I watch from the deck instead as they struggle with brotherhood.

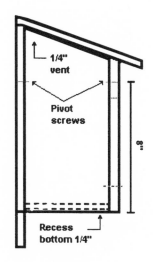

They are safe enough here, I think. Our locks protect us. The pretend boundaries of our property lines protect us. We know that isn't entirely true, but at the time I felt all those things. My wife has started another project inside, and soon the sun will begin to set and I will call the boys in, lock the doors. And when the paint is fully dried, I will hang the rocket birdhouse from the tree, safely away from brush and other attractions for wrens and swallows.

When I began searching for a bird enclosure for my boys to make, I thought about what kind of a home I was getting. What kind of domicile. But it didn't take me long to realize that the thicket of grass and feather and needle were temporary lodgings, and no matter how long I might stay, a hotel simply wouldn't ever be home.

Somehow, a rocket seemed just right.

from *The Homeowner's Guide to Deer Prevention*

I collected the cut hair of our youngest into a cup. It was fine, and though it clumped into thick braids for a short time, it soon divested itself of companionship and became a nest. My wife spread the baby-hair clippings around the garden to keep away the deer, a slip of air heartstringing them along the tree line.

> *Other techniques observed: hanging soap cakes with drill-press signatures roped about the branches of the orchard trees, the curlings slick and fine in the cuffs of pants. Children potty training in the backyard. A yappy dog, whirligigs, and scarecrows. Lavender, sage, thyme, bottlebrush, carpet bugle, wisteria. Pepper flakes and cayenne.*

A small town circumscribed by woods, the center of our village is another large wooded area. It is no surprise the deer venture out. They wander the town cemetery at night, they nuzzle along the fence lines in the twilight. Once, taking out the trash, I found four young adult deer staggered from my front yard to the street as though they were posing for an album cover. They wandered a night apart. We knew they'd visit—the missing heads of perennials, the light touch of hoof to unmulched garden dirt.

Deer are clumsy when they are slow, as though their throttle were squelched. I watched two adolescents feed on grass outside my office window at a colony, and saw the way they ticked and jolted, hooves boosted high in the grass. Then a car passed on the road, and only a moment of hesitation before they were gone. What it must feel like to have the speed and leap of a stag. The youth too. First you are frozen in a stare, and then speed is just a blur of limbs.

> *The Celts called them fairy cattle and held them as known associates of deities. The antlers have held a crucifix known to help convert Saint Hubertus to Christianity. He is the patron saint of, among other things, hunters.*

My aunt tells the story of when she wrecked her car in high school, having fallen asleep at the wheel. She woke to a deer head staring through the windshield, the neck contorted unbelievably toward her, and she passed out again until a state trooper woke her in the morning. The pupil of a deer's eye is a horizontal ellipse, the better to see periphery, their tapetum lucidum reflecting light, a mirror. When the eyes looked at her, she had no choice but to see herself.

> *On the New York State Highways, an average of twenty thousand deer carcasses are collected and disposed of each year. The peak time for this collection is fall and early winter. There are 1.5 million deer-related accidents in the United States, according to the National Highway Traffic Safety*

Administration. Deterrents for deer on highways: slower speed limits; whistlers mounted on cars; solar-powered subsonic noisemakers and strobe lights.

It is magical to think that a bit of hair would work. The deer have recently been eating the tops of the lilies too tall for bunnies. It is time for another haircut for my son. The work has been hard in the garden. The world is an ellipse to deer. An orbit. Your pleasures are not their pleasures. Your scent is dry ice, and all they know is that with which you fill their nose.

Wind Turbine

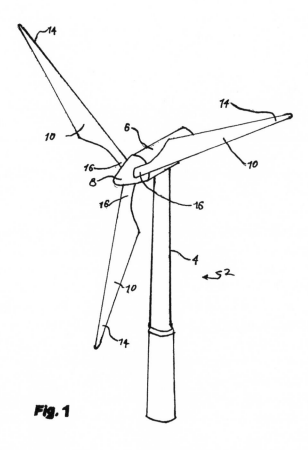

Fig. 1

2. Outside of Ellsworth, Kansas, at dusk a fire ranged over 80 acres. We were in our van driving to my parents' house, the end of a very long trip across the country, and we watched out the windows as a line of fire cleared the stubble from a harvested field. Interstate 70 winds around a series of hills in that area, the road cut into the granite, and we could just still see the striations by the dwindling light.

4. Half an hour of orange and yellow rubbed against the evening horizon line like smoky resin, and the fire sliced the encroaching darkness like an open parenthetical. The rest of the landscape was a flat, dark disc against the horizon line. My boys, leaning across the back seat to see the fire, were speechless.

6. The survival speed of a wind turbine is the maximum speed a turbine can spin without being damaged. Built into the nacelle are brakes, a full set of gears, and a slow speed shaft to keep the blades from accruing too much force. Each blade weighs 27,000 pounds and is 173 feet long. The momentum they produce is staggering.

8. My wife and I were in the midst of a disagreement when we came upon the fire. I'd done something stupid and wasn't about to admit it. I could feel I was wrong, but instead of apologizing I grew defensive and silent. The boys continued to watch the fire in silence behind us.

10. Some of my greatest regrets are my ill-advised silences.

14. The fire passed, and we cleared the final curve in the road. Over the hill a cluster of wind turbines spiraled the sky. Against the diminishing sun they were da Vinci's Vitruvian Man. Rotors worked

to wipe the sky clean of its resin. We could hear the distortion of air. There were too many to count, and they towered 400 feet above us like gods.

16. Even with the blades shuttered, a Kansas wind can spin the blades off a wind turbine like tearing a kite from a string. The true measure of a well-constructed wind turbine is how well the brakes keep the violent speed in check. How to take energy from the air with a slow spin that looks effortless. Mile after mile there were wind turbines until we could no longer see them due to darkness. It was a calm night, and only right then I felt a love in the van, my boys submitting to sleep, my wife needing my voice in the darkness pulling us back to ourselves.

X-Ray Machine

My oldest son told me his first lie. He was six, and at six he was easy to crack. His lie covered up hitting his brother. He stood in his pajamas, near his cabinet of books, as he does when he's done something wrong, the cabinet a waterfall of books coming unhinged from their shelves. Screaming ensues when they must share and when they must divide. They trade punches like drunken sailors over a quarter-machine rubber ball. There will be no more books or games, I say. Not unless you apologize.

· · ·

I'm thinking of the game *Operation*, a game we gave the boys for Christmas. The aim to avoid touching the sides of the open wound as the various organs and objects are extracted from the body, yet they delight in the buzzing, in the wrongness of it. I watch them, their anticipation growing, and when the buzzer goes off, they squeal.

· · ·

One can build a homemade x-ray machine with fairly simplistic technological skill. A radio tube, copper wire, mixing bowls, and lead sheathing. Plastic and magnetic wire. Varnished cambric. It can take out a city block of televisions and radios. It can fry a person. You can find the details online.

. . .

When a child gets an x-ray, he stands in front of a target. Crosshairs, a muzzle firing particles aimed at his chest. They put a full-length body shield on observers, parents, and the weight drags shoulders down. But there in its sights the boy stands, brave against the firing.

. . .

John Spinello designed an electrified box and metal connector game for a college class in 1962. The game was polished by Milton Bradley, with "Cavity Sam" and the famous body parts, in '65 and given the name *Operation*. Spinello received five hundred dollars and the promise of a job he never got after college. *Operation* is one of the most successful games Milton Bradley has ever produced.

. . .

There is a buzzing sound that accompanies the x-ray fish on the toy my youngest son spins. The base and sides are white, and at any time the spinning center might land on CAT or ELEPHANT. But he most often stops it at X-RAY FISH, listens to the electrocution sound like the noise from Dr. Frankenstein's laboratory, and then his eager hand spins it again.

. . .

The x-ray fish, or *Pristella maxillaris*, is transparent. Like those deep-sea creatures that haven't bothered to hide their insides, because what is the point of skin if the eyes don't pry? Unlike the gelatinous deep-sea jellies, however, these fish have light rib bones and swim outside the midnight zone. The x-ray fish is in a perpetual state of examination, unable to lie about its mystery.

. . .

I can see what my son has done wrong, and the lie he used to cover it up. It is an innocent lie, but he is transparent because even a simple gaze forces the truth from him, and he admits to the hitting and offers himself up to the time-out chair. The x-ray machine, I always imagined, looked right through you. But I was wrong. It only looks far enough inside to see what doesn't belong.

Come Celebrate the Radial Arm Saw

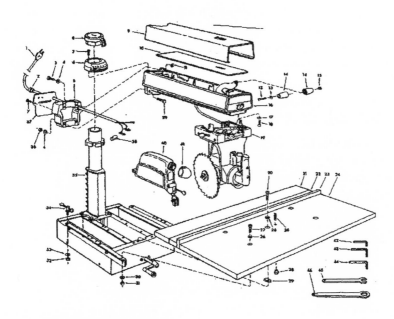

1. I could piddle all day like this
2. using my radial arm saw
3. and the whole while saying "radial arm saw"
4. like a line of poetry
5. but it's a machine
6. I know all too well the power and danger

7. so chanting the line as I rip a plywood board
8. into two-foot-wide strips to become the sides of a carcass
9. becomes a constant warning
10. an oral and auditory awareness
11. of the spinning tooth metal
12. I constantly push toward and pull from
13. to create these bookshelves and lowboys and end tables
14. and building so I don't have to buy them
15. sure but also because wood is better than pressed wood
16. and my sons will see that I made these
17. or be told sure
18. and that I'm losing this ability as I do it less often sure
19. and it is something
20. one small thing
21. I might be able to pass on perhaps
22. that I might do when this whole academic structure comes tumbling down
23. maybe
24. and this saw which was my father's radial arm saw
25. was purchased the year I was born
26. which he used at night
27. after the full days on location as an oil-field hand
28. imagine him
29. wilted from the sun and the day
30. he still heard the bowing grains whisper

31. wanting him to rub them with his fingers and trim them down
    some
32. just so
33. to make quick work of their splinters
34. and maybe
35. perhaps
36. this is the best reason
37. to build this carcass I'm now gluing in place
38. and securing with vice and clamp
39. because this saw and I are the same age
40. we both have worn teeth and a motor that has seen better days
41. and I can come out here
42. to this cold garage to chant
43. and we can warm it up some with spent electricity
44. sawdust and hopes of a straight line.
45. Because my dad gave me this radial arm saw.
46. Because he expected I would use it.

Solomon Grundy Says Good Night

My sons play a new game, holding on to my legs, standing on my feet as I lumber them to bed. My legs are stiff and I am now Solomon Grundy, the comic book monster. They delight in monsters and insist on a ride to the bathroom, to the bedroom, to the kitchen for a drink. They are blindly confident in me. They do not know how little balance I have. Solomon Grundy is my youngest son's favorite monster—he who was brought back to the living by a swamp. I do his voice from the cartoon, a little deep Louisiana mixed with an unmodulated tenor, and he squeals with delight. I walk like him, the boys attached, my hands pretending to tickle but actually holding them, my palms able to cup nearly the entirety of their backs. What my boys don't know is there are real monsters out there that don't lumber slowly. They have not come back from the dead.

Bela Lugosi inadvertently created Frankenstein's monster's iconic walk when filmmakers had to fix the problem of his accent, essentially eliminating all his speaking parts. In one of those speaking parts, he explains through monologue that in a previous movie, the monster has lost his sight, and as a result he walked in a shuffle, his arms forward. Zombies, mummies, the resurrected dead of this world, they are discovering, all carry this same gait. They all stumble, slowly, with weak legs and suspect balance. They often use their arms, forward, to keep themselves upright. They seem to be longing, reaching infinitely. They don't have language. Modern monsters brought back from the dead no longer walk that way because of blindness, they walk that way because they carry an immense weight on their backs, their chests, their stiff, unbending legs. They carry it until they feel like they might not be able to carry it any longer, then they carry it some more.

Solomon Grundy say good night to the little boys, I say. I deposit them in bed. Funny, they don't have nightmares. They keep asking for more, but I bend from the knees to kiss them good night. There is no greater joy than their laughter before bed, and every night I realize I can shoulder it no longer.

The Arrow of Time

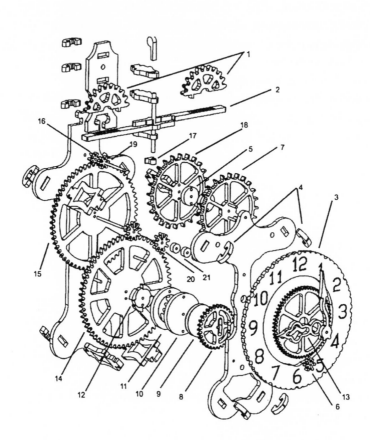

1. Each clock gives me a different reading.
2. Some are set to summertime, some to the winter.
3. These are battery-powered and fall back or spring forward with the dial behind the face.
4. The one in our bathroom is five minutes fast.
5. The oven and the microwave are always flashing, and we have stopped setting them.
6. The coffee maker is missing segments of the numbers, so we do not know if it is set to the right time. We suspect not, so we do not schedule coffee.
7. The bedside clock in the guest room has not been used since my mother-in-law's last visit, and so is set to summertime. It continues to lose time since her return to Florida.
8. My phone and my wife's phone and my computer all read the same. They are set by the Network Time Protocol based on Coordinated Universal Time.
9. There are three clocks in the basement. Each ticks, and each tick offset but also measuring different second-lengths.
10. How is that possible?
11. The back of the basement, my office, must be some sort of minor black hole, time lengthening, where I try to remember the past and fail miserably, all my memories needing fact-checkers.
12. My Swatch is stuck in its own time in the early nineties. My Citizen needs motion, and thus has stopped at 6:43.
13. My grandfather's old pocket watch, which he gave me, no longer keeps time, the glass shattered.

14. He's gone now, and every year on his birthday I think about going to a jeweler to have it refurbished.
15. My oldest son can tell time, so for Christmas we bought him a watch. It has a Lego character embedded in the red, blue, and yellow band, and I adjust it by taking out one of the two extra heads. He takes it off every chance he gets, choosing to fiddle with time between his fingers.
16. Finally, there's the projection clock in my boys' room.
17. It's a rocket.
18. It shows pictures of the solar system on the ceiling, where a humidifier will draw forth small oily golden domes leeched from the paint.
19. At night the pictures fade, but with the push of a button time hovers there, and none of us care if it's the right time. We are all launched into sleep like an arrow toward the future.
20. In our house there's always a ticking clock, but in sleep clocks don't matter.
21. Our boys don't wake in the night, and so we live in wintertime and summertime and nightmare-time and past-time and pleasure-time, and in all-these-times our alarms will wake us.

Geode

I must have cracked about twenty geodes at my sons' birthday party. I selected a small finish hammer and tapped the geodes lightly but regularly along a line like an equator, turning and tapping, turning and tapping. Inside were the dirty brown crystals of the common geode. Some broke in a simple half, along a line I followed, but others burst forth their crystals in fragments. I thought this might disappoint the children, but the shards delighted them, and I began to think something inside of them desired the breaking apart. Where were the exotic purple crystals the directions suggested might be there? I tapped and another was thrust at me. I tapped the rock, trying to expose the crystalized gas trapped in the volcanic residue so many years before. It was midsummer, the boys and girls holding their rocks with the promise that their geode would be the one especially for them. And my sons, I could see them as adults thumbing their shards of geode in a pocket, some charm they kept for the rest of their lives. And their wives making sure it didn't get tossed in a can with the rest of the change at the end of the day, and their kids, someday, years later, tapping at my arm and shoulder to open them up a geode, and I'd gladly take up the hammer and split myself apart to see what crystal metastasized and oh their delight not at my simple splitting but at my bursting forth.

from *The Suitor's Almanac*

Suitor's Rain: June 1–September 30 [Philippines–Florida]

It was raining in Florida, and my mother-in-law told me about the suitor's rain, the rain that kept a suitor from leaving after he had called on a young woman. If timed perfectly, the suitor could not be denied dinner in the Philippines, and it was often the young woman's grandmother, she told me, that scolded *Will he really stay for dinner? Can he not walk home?*

It was raining in Florida every afternoon at the same time, and so we arranged to be home. My sons crawled the walls, and we took long naps when the afternoon rains came. The whole house shut down like a heavy eyelid, the sound of water in our hair and fingers. When we woke it was suppertime.

I asked her whether she'd ever been a victim of the suitor's rain, and she told me she'd never been so fortunate. *My sisters*, she told me, *I think there were boys who watched the sky to come see them.* Her home was covered in Legos and Hot Wheels cars. My youngest pulled her letter-writing materials from her small desk and hid all her pens. He fought with my oldest for rights to nap with his *lola*.

In the afternoons the rain fell so hard one might worry for the integrity of the shingles on the roof. Orchids hung in small baskets from trees.

Anoles and skinks latched to her screened-in porch and the branches of her fruit trees, prized possessions grown from seed brought here from Kerala and Bolinao—papaya, mango, jackfruit, lychee. Her white and red orange trees. Inside her cuttings, all along the edges of her porch, are surprise frogs the size of thumbnails. The boys get as close to the hanging lizards as they can, reaching out to touch. Then, the scoot and tick whisk the lizards to a safe corner.

Some days we loaded up and went an hour west to the beach, where the coast at least tempered the heat. Or half an hour north to the mall and its air conditioning. Anywhere but outside in central Florida, where the heat and humidity cleared the streets. On the day she told that story, though, we stayed in. The boys read and played on the couch. My father-in-law was off to work, and my wife and I relaxed with magazines, enjoying the lack of a schedule. There was a baseball game on, and my mother-in-law kept one eye on the game, another on preparing *lumpia* for dinner. The rain was falling, and it would continue to fall throughout the evening.

Monsoon Season—June 5–October 30 [India—variable]

Like coming up for air a fraction of a second too late, and taking in some of the water from the pool—that coughing and gasping before recovery. That feeling, for an hour in the hottest part of the day.

Hurricane Season—June 1–November 30 [Florida]

In 2004 two hurricanes crossed the main body of Florida. The point of conjunction—where the two paths crossed—is where my in-laws live. Hurricane Charley made landfall on August 13, a Friday, and Hurricane Frances came on September 5. In between were tropical storm Bonnie and Hurricanes Jeanne and Ivan.

My mother-in-law spent a couple of long nights in the bathtub with her cockatiel Chico, the rain beating the roof and the walls. She said the house shook with the force of the winds. Her husband, a respiratory therapist, was stuck at the hospital in Wauchula, where the power went off for several hours and they relied on backup generators. This was Hurricane Charley, the first storm that made landfall and then abruptly turned inland against the predictions of meteorologists.

The names make a hurricane seem like what it is, a living thing. But the name also provides a feeling that the body count it racks up might be somehow easier to manage. Charley did it, after all, not some weather system.

We lost contact with my wife's family for a time. We were a wreck, helpless, watching for news of the landfall on television. My mother-in-law with candles lit, power out, listening to the hurricanes knocking and knocking and not coming in.

Tornado Season—March 1-August 30 [Kansas—variable]

There are too many windows in my parents' home. There are too many stories to their home. There are too few points of egress. There is stained glass. How many tornadoes have we seen form over us? We walk outside when the horns blast because seeing it coming makes it less frightening.

They formed before us when I was a child. My memory of this is clear, sitting on the back deck, looking westward, seeing funnel clouds form near Ellis, Kansas, like a straw dropped in a glass of dishwater. This memory is manufactured: they crossed along the skyline writing their names on the fields and towns and homes below. Tornado dancers. Multiple touchdowns.

Dirt devils rising from the ground, a magician's trick. My memory is a dirt devil rising fast and hard, eighty acres away, as I drove a tractor for a farmer for the first and only time. I stopped the tractor to watch, got out and took a piss near the tractor tire. The dust thick at the base of the dirty swirl, a needle rising from it, lifting higher. Never seen one this big.

Reports of a tornado pulling up corn in Nebraska, the stalks and ears and leaves of the corn finally descending later that day in Kansas.

Our home with its windows and its poor-latching screen doors. There are too many sharp objects. Too many trees with loose branches. Too many too many.

When I returned home my family told me a tornado had touched ground west of town. Near the field and the tractor. Near me. Did I see it, they asked. I said yes, but I can't know for sure. Too much dust and fresh-turned soil. I won't ever know.

Hurricane Season—June 1–November 30 [Saint Lucia]

Rain steps into our room through the missing fourth wall. Rain can only tiptoe, does not know the heels of its feet. The soft pad-pad upon the tile floor sounds like a prayer as we wake. We look out on the Piton Mountains as the rain lifts a fog from them, from us, and I fall again to sleep. Later, in the first rain forest I've ever visited, I don't get wet despite the constant rain. The rain waits outside the canopy, knocks in its breathy way to come in. I touch a crab claw flower, red and curling, and something taps me on the shoulder: rain's reminder that there is so much more to see. I listen to the rain and move down the path. Any direction we go, the rain is a denizen holding our hands.

I would like to climb the rain as though it were a ladder with the tiniest wet rungs. Remember the brick home whose floor had been uprooted by a tree? The tree now grows from its family room, its canopy covering what the roof had long since abandoned. Had the family fallen asleep at the tree's trunk? Had they carved their names into the bark, rubbed it clean with their backs? The east wall vanished, the other three intact. Branches shed rain, and the only way to reach the top of the tree would be to climb the spiraling staircase that caressed the leaves, slid from the tips, and cascaded to the floor below.

The Gun and the Bird

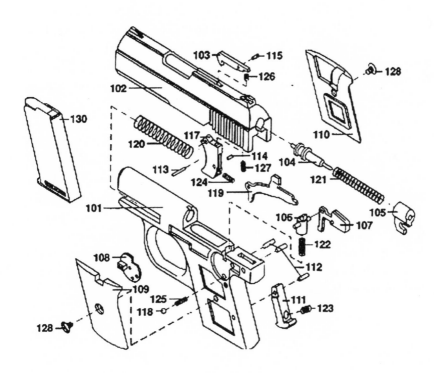

101. I sat down at the landlord's table rife with papers and takeout and plates and cups. It is forgivable I might not see, beneath a dirty magazine, the bulge of a pistol.

102. His apartment, the ground floor beneath his tenants, was a single subscription to *Playboy* away from total suffocation.

103. The lone end table in his studio apartment contained the Tower of Babel of contracts and notices.

104. His own health seemed to ebb with the heat and whether his window AC might shoot craps.

105. It was, in short, a shit hole.

106. And that made me more nervous. In the past few minutes, he'd been asking me whether I knew how hard it was to be a landlord.

107. "People think you'll just give up, you know?"

108. I'd just clipped his car on the street out front running an errand, and two of his tenants told me where the man lived.

109. Then he uncovered the .25 caliber pocket pistol.

110. The gun did not rest on the table. It balanced there.

111. It was small like a toy.

112. I'd never seen a gun so carelessly kept.

113. The metal corroded, the brown plastic grip broken—excavated from the earth that very morning by the look of it.

114. He was talking about rent.

115. About people cheating him.

117. He hardly looked at the gun when he pulled the magazine away. But he had my eye, and he knew it.

118. "The guys that rent here? You gotta be careful."

119. The two men that directed me to his door were rough-looking characters by their scars. Their faces held a morning bake and buzz that they might have felt requisite to get through their day.

120. I had to wonder at that moment why he was showing me this gun.

121. I posed no threat in my khaki shorts and T-shirt.

122. I'd come to his door, my insurance information already written down on the piece of paper I handed to him.

123. I didn't suggest in any way that what he was saying might be wrong, or that I didn't believe him.

124. Ego? His means seemed to suggest that he didn't need to prove anything.

125. Maybe he wanted to teach a soft man a lesson about the hard side of town.

126. I stood, and made my excuses to leave.

127. "I appreciate your honesty," he said. "I'll call your agent."

128. I exited to the sidewalk and hurried to my van. The scratches on both our vehicles were superficial, and the repairs for him would be of the most minor inconvenience if he chose to fix them at all.

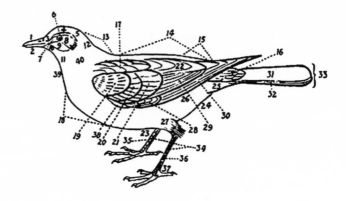

1–5.   It was during this time that a misguided robin began his crusade to enter our bathroom through the opaque window near our shower.

6–12.   For several days in the afternoons, when the brightest sun might make that window appear as a mirror, he charged the window, causing a *thud!* that roused me from bed.

13–17.   He sat on a lilac just a few yards from the window.

18.   The leaves were just emerging, the warmth of the afternoon magnified by the windows in the house for the first time in a long winter.

19–22.   My boys were to make a scarecrow on paper to tape to the window.

23–25.   I was going to set chimes on the lilac.

26–30.   *Thud!*

31–33. The profile of the bird with full wingspan where he pulled away from the glass, just a fuzzy outline.

34–36. *Thud!*

37. I was startled by the contact.

38. I was thinking of the gun.

39. *Thud!*

40. And then he stopped. He went away. Maybe he thought he defeated his foe.

From a Rooftop

1. We do not expect flight without feathers, but here come the bats nonetheless, an air parade of points and skin and fur.
2. It is dusk, and they come from their day roost in squadrons.
3. These brown bats are not lucky enough to have a bat house, so they roost in a hollow rotting tree in a neighboring yard.
4. They come to these hunting grounds.
5. Standing water in wet summers like a farm-to-table restaurant in a small Parisian town.
6. Near this man, who is alone atop his house cleaning his gutters.
7. It's a simple ranch with a light pitch, and this man has unreliable knees.
8. He isn't as agile as he once was.
9. The ears of the brown bat are small, the eyes smaller.
10. The squeak issued from their mouths registers as the hint of sound to a human.
11. Their wings so large they fold in on themselves.
12. Terrestrially miserable, aeronautically simple.
13. It is a bat's mammalian weight that makes it possible, cutting corners faster than any bird can, the muscles so flexible they enjoy a contortionist's labyrinth of the body.
14. Slow motion shows the common bat able to retract one wing independently, using speed and drag to swing itself on currents to capture the next buzzing morsel on a warm summer night.
15. In real time at dusk, seeing a bat awing is seeing shadows in peripheral vision.

16. Small dark figures unmistakably cut and flit near, but they can't be seen directly.
17. They are the suggestion of form.
18. Close your eyes and imagine being fast enough to blur the eye.
19. Imagine hearing so keen images appear in the mind.
20. Imagine catching food in midair, like popcorn tossed above an open mouth.
21. Imagine never missing.
22. It's a memory of a rooftop patio dinner in Paris,
23. bread and cheese all that could be afforded,
24. spread across the table,
25. hands and butter knives everywhere,
26. a spilled drink, another bottle,
27. take it from the pile of francs there sir
28. we don't know what the value is but we trust you
29. and we'll stay here and drink and eat
30. until the francs are gone
31. and don't forget to take a little for yourself.
32. We're young and agile
33. and we'll hawk and glean until the morning
34. and find our roost, our hibernaculum,
35. and our dreams will be of the air, of the night,
36. of hearing so keen,
37. of taste so acute,
38. it forms an outline in our minds.

Sandhill Cranes

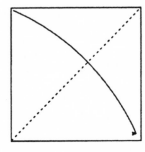

1.

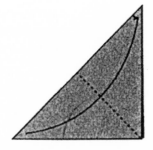

2.

Ten thousand sandhill cranes
erupted when they gathered
together.

Nebraska fields along the
Platte River teemed with
their red button eyes.

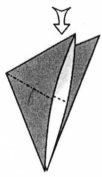

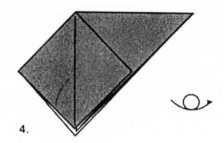

3.

I froze in a blind for hours, awaited their arrival only to hear them before I could see them.

4.

For a few minutes sound was tactile.

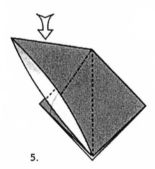

5.

Thousands of sonic booms called *garoo-a-a-a*, just like *Peterson's Field Guide* told me they would.

6.

A riot of white and gray stretching after grain left in the fields.

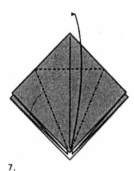

7.

I learned that the cranes have made this migratory trip for millions of years, guided by something we don't yet completely understand.

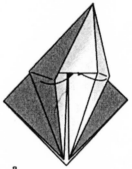

8.

A professor who came along on the trip also taught us our basic stargazing, locating Arcturus, showing us how to navigate by the stars.

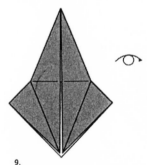

9.

Seventeen years later, married with children, on a visit to my in-laws in Florida we saw three cranes browsing sweetgrass near a small lake.

10.

My son's instinct was to rush them.

11.

I knelt down and told him
these birds came from Canada,
thousands of miles, to be here.

12.

I'd seen ten thousand at once,
I said.

13.

These three spread their wings
and hopped away, skittish.

14.

One shrill bugle and my son
asked, "Are these the only ones
that made it?"

15.

Suddenly all those years disappeared and I remembered thinking again about the North Star.

16.

That night, in Nebraska, after we'd looked at the stars, we could all hear the gurgle of the nesting birds.

17.

All these years later, I thought I knew they all made it. I was almost certain I could tell my son these might be the same ones from so many years ago. Then, suddenly, they flew off. We watched them, long bodies like an arrow, and we didn't make a sound.

How to Make a Cardinal in Five Easy Steps

Step 1

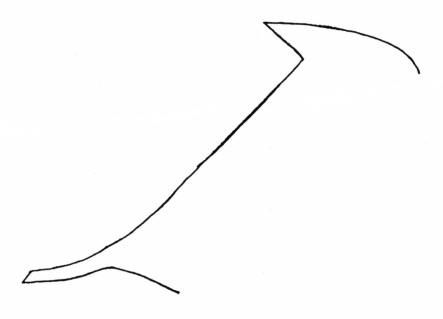

Step 1:

Your sons have known their colors for as long as they could talk. Your wife shares their names with the boys: periwinkle, magenta, coral, café au lait. Before your youngest could talk he could identify chartreuse.

Blue, you might say.

Turquoise, Dad, is their answer.

You might consider your color palette as the opening strokes of a simple drawing: straight lines and basic representations. Color was a thing artists needed. You didn't think they had consequences. Your world was homogenous, and you were unaware of the effect color could have on a life.

Your entire family has an eye for color that you simply don't have. You're not color-blind, but your gradations of hue are not in the "gifted" range. Color seemed like the result of measures outside your control. You could see light and dark green, for instance, but to say that this light green is *emerald* not only would be outside your abilities, but would simply never occur to you.

Obviously it is because it never has had to.

Step 2

Step 2:

One can be trained to see different shades of color and to identify them. One can train an eye like training a muscle, by repetition and through difficulty. But eventually, the eye can make judgments on hue and tone that it simply didn't have the capacity to do before.

Draw the wing—it will be the first difficult thing you do. There are variations on the size of the plumes, the heft and width of the patagium.

You make missteps. You call something one color, and it is not. You minimize the importance of getting a color correct, and you remember that it matters to those you talk to. It should also matter to you. You hope you handle these missteps gracefully, but you know there are times where you simply don't.

But people are patient. That might be the one thing you never really knew until you began trying to understand color. There is a flexibility in the way people live in their world. Sometimes, when you think they should contract away from you, they expand instead in welcome.

Step 3

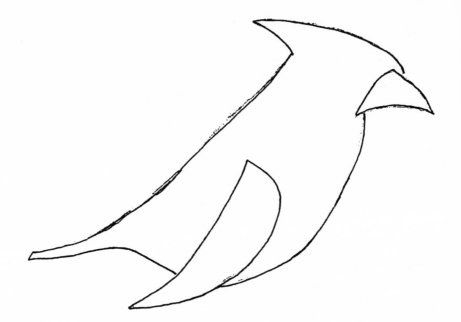

Step 3:

Your youngest son drew a picture of himself as a prince at school. You see it first on the wall of other little princes in his classroom, and it is beautiful, and you wonder at his ability to capture his own likeness at such a young age. Your wife—who sometimes used to worry that he didn't understand his heritage, that he would "forget" to say to those who might ask that he is half Asian American, that it would be "too much" for a first grader to say that he is one-quarter south Indian and one-quarter Filipino—doesn't find the drawing at first when she scans the bulletin board, but is overjoyed once she locks her eyes on it to see that he has used a brown crayon to color himself.

Your job is to help him know these things too. But you realize your sons understand these color variations much more swiftly and easily than you do.

Finish the body by drawing a beak just below the cap and bringing the chest up to the beak. You've got the whole *object* of the bird now. It is identifiable as a bird, like it could be used on a street sign to signify BIRD.

You and your wife kept the picture, and when you see it you can't help but be sad, not that he's used a color that accurately captures his own skin, but that you know he is growing up and grasping *color* in a bigger sense. You are sad because you don't know what this means for him.

Step 4

Step 4:

Nobody has ever asked you what you are. Nobody has ever stumbled over your name. Nobody has ever called you a derogatory term. Nobody has ever stopped what they were doing to look at you when you walked in a room you were expected to be in. Nobody has called you exotic. Nobody has ever jeered. Nobody has ever whispered. Nobody cuts you off when you are talking. Nobody makes you wait. Nobody has denied you an opportunity. Nobody has truly feared you, with or without reason.

Draw the mask for the bird.

Step 5

Step 5:

The juvenile male cardinal, until adult maturity, will resemble the mother. You'll be relieved to know that this protects the juvenile cardinal from harm and allows him to mature. There is a beauty in this shade too.

Draw the details. The legs upon which he will stand, the branch upon which he will perch. Finish his beak, the better for him to speak.

Before he develops the flamboyant cap and burns a bright red, he is his mother's shadow. He understands at an early age his mother's world. Thank God, the adult male cardinal thinks, awing, gathering and foraging. Thank God for that.

Duck Call

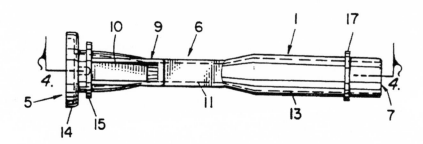

1. Bless the duck in her nest and the mallard who protects her or tries to
4. bless the grass she swirls to nest
5. bless the spread of feathers and the patch of grass she found surrounded by
6. bless the water running in the river
7. bless the sound that blankets
9. bless the slap squeak
10. bless it covers the drama
11. bless the nest and the eyes

13. bless from the bridge where we
14. bless the songs we hear
15. bless the flight from water like an arrow
17. bless the mess of our lives

ACKNOWLEDGMENTS

Essays from this manuscript were previously published, sometimes in different forms, in the following publications: "Book of Ghosts" (as "Ghosts in the Essay") appeared on *Essay Daily*; "Pumpjack" (#1) appeared in *DIAGRAM*; "Harvest" appeared in *Seneca Review*; "Exploded View" appeared in *Em: A Review of Text + Image*; "Mulberries" and "Transmission" appeared in *Sugared Water*; "Jackfruit" and "X-Ray Machine" appeared in *Pleiades*; "Fruit Fly Extermination" and "Geode" appeared in *Masque and Spectacle*; "from *The Homeowner's Guide to Deer Prevention*" appeared in *The Collagist*; "from *The Suitor's Almanac*" appeared in *Fugue*; "The Owl in Twenty-Six Folds" appeared in *Natural Bridge*; "Mousetrap" appeared in *Normal School: Online Supplement Summer 2015* and is reprinted by permission of *The Normal School*, Copyright 2015 by Dustin Parsons; "The Graduates of Fly-Fishing School, Sarasota, Florida, Class of June 13, 2013" appeared in *New Delta Review*; "The Festive Revolver" appeared in *Zone 3*; "Drop Off" appeared in *Indiana Review*; "Pumpjack" (#2) appeared in *Crab Orchard Review*; "Come Celebrate the Radial Arm Saw," "Fujita Scale," and "Wind Turbine" appeared in *Passages North*; "Take an Island, Give an Island Back" appeared in *Proximity*; "from *Stories I've Been Told: Student*" (as "When I Asked a Student to Tell Me a Story") and "Duck Call" appeared in *Jelly*

Bucket; "Silhouettes" appeared in *Stone Canoe*; "The Flood Plain" is forthcoming in *Hotel Amerika*.

The images for my project were drawn from various found sources. Patent drawings include those on pages 1 (pumpjack, 1973), 47 (integration of a solar panel into a mobile touchscreen device with a flexible display, 2016), 49 (solar energy converting apparatus, 1957), 54 (a tornado graph for the method of determining formation resistivity utilizing combined measurements of inductive and galvanic logging instruments), 91 (mousetrap, 2003), 155 (wind turbine, 2011), and 198 (duck call, 1979). Other images were drawn from instruction manuals and guides, online and in print, including those on pages 6, 8, and 10 (free online instructions for steel shed construction at http://scianda.blogspot.com); 107–13 (step-by-step instructions for owl origami from www.origami-resource-center .com); 144–51 (bluebird house instructions from New York State Bluebird Society free-use plans); and 183–87 (step-by-step instructions for crane origami from www.origami-resource-center.com). Detailed parts diagrams were another major resource, as appear on pages 29 (exploded view of a 1988 Nissan pickup manual transmission from www.autozone .com); 36 (flatbed truck from www.boulderarts.net), 44 (exploded view of the Solar Tracker from Science and Education Publishing at www.pubs .sciepub.com), 139 (Steyr-Hahn M.1911 & M.1912 Pistol from www .warrelics.eu), 141 (compass from DSG Aviation. Used with permission); 161 (radial arm saw from Sears Craftsman manual, 1973), 166 (clock from www.sinequanon.wordpress.com), and 175 (Raven25-caliber pistol from http://jtjersey.com). Scientific identification guides and texts provided another resource, as on pages 42 and 50 (dog show diagram from *Solving the Mysteries of Breed Type* by Richard G. Beauchamp [Allenhurst, N.J.: Kennel Club Books, 2008]); 52–53 (bird identification silhouettes from *A Field Guide to the Birds of Eastern and Central North America*, 5th ed., by Roger Tony Peterson. Illustrations copyright © 2002 by Marital Trust B. u/a Roger Tory Peterson. Reprinted by permission of Houghton Mifflin Harcourt Publishing Company. All rights reserved); 71, 73, 75, 77, and 80 (flood plain production, source unknown); 99–102 (animal prints from www.123rf.com); and 178 (bird from *British Birds and Their Eggs*, by J. Maclair Boraston, 1909). Maps came from various other sources; they include those images appearing on pages 38 (map of southwest Kansas from Bowling Green State University Libraries) and 120–22 and 124–25 (map of Hundred Islands, Philippines, from www.tourism-philippines .com). The image on page 180 is a connect-the-dots bat from www .coloring.ws. The other drawings are my own, as appear on pages 40 (house layout); 82, 84, and 86 (parts of a book); and 188, 190, 192, 194, and 196 (cardinal drawing instructions).

I'd like to thank my agent, Christopher Rhodes, for standing by a weird little project.

Thank you to all the editors who helped me create magic out of these images and words, especially Ander Monson, Phil Memmer, Maggie Messitt, Steven Church, Matthew Gavin Frank, Phong Nguyen, Allison Joseph and Jon Tribble, Amy Wright, Shane Seely, Heather Momyer, Craig Reinbold, and John D'Agata. Thanks to all the editors and designers at the University of Georgia Press, including Erin Kirk New, Jon Davies, Walter Biggins, Beth Snead, Lisa Bayer, and especially John Griswold. And to the talents of Jennifer Comeau. I'm eternally grateful.

My heart also goes out to all my colleagues in Mississippi who, just by surrounding me with their good hearts and art, make me a better writer: Beth Ann Fennelly, Tom Franklin, Derrick Harriell, Melissa Ginsburg, Chris Offutt, Kiese Laymon, and Matt Bondurant.

Birger, Iclal, Emily, Scott: All my love and appreciation.

Without support from Ivo Kamps and the University of Mississippi, this book would never have been assembled. Thank you so much!

Thanks to the Vermont Studio Center and the Brush Creek Foundation for the Arts for hosting me in two magnificent residencies where a lot of this work was done.

Finally, none of this is possible without family support. Thank you to Max and Karen Parsons: even though my nose was in a book most of the time, I was always watching you for examples of how to love. Thanks to Mathew and Paz Nezhukumatathil for their support and help, and for offering up stories and ideas, even when they didn't know they were doing it.

Thanks to my boys, Pascal and Jasper, for making me a better man. I hope this book reflects even a fraction of the pride I have in your golden hearts.

Aimee Nezhukumatathil, you are the beating heart of this book. You believed this could be a book when I simply didn't. You were always right. I could never have done this without you, Aimee.